Interesting Facts

For Adults

Crafted by Skriuwer

Introduction

Welcome to a journey through 2000+ interesting facts that will spark your curiosity and broaden your understanding of the world. This book dives into a wide range of topics, offering a treasure chest of information from ancient times to modern days, the natural world to the supernatural, and everyday life to extraordinary events. Discover the remains of ancient civilizations, uncover mysteries that have puzzled experts for years, and marvel at achievements that have set world records. Learn about amazing inventions that changed history, see the incredible natural events on our planet, and relive important historical events that shaped our world.

Get to know famous people who left their mark on history, explore the vast reaches of space, and learn about unusual animals that seem out of this world. Dive into myths and legends that have fascinated cultures for centuries, and uncover hidden places that remain unknown to many. This book also highlights rare diseases that challenge doctors, architectural wonders that show human creativity, and cultural traditions that celebrate the diversity of human life. You will travel through different countries and languages, encounter strange laws that are hard to believe, and understand the science experiments that expanded our knowledge.

From geographical oddities and paranormal activities to lost cities and forgotten technologies, each page promises surprises and learning. Explore facts about the human body, enjoy the diversity of food and drink, and appreciate the artistic and literary works that define our culture. Understand psychological phenomena that explain human behavior, feel the thrill of extreme sports, and study cryptozoology's search for legendary creatures. Theories of time travel, infamous heists, language quirks, and historical battles are all part of this rich collection. Discover the lives of notorious pirates, inventive hoaxes, and space mysteries that intrigue scientists.

Ancient artifacts, superstitions, and the secrets of historical figures add depth to our understanding of the past. Engage with themes of exploration and discovery, hidden histories, medical breakthroughs, and psychic phenomena that challenge our views. Rare collectibles, artistic techniques, and global festivals showcase human creativity and celebration. Military innovations, technology advancements, and movie trivia reveal our pursuit of progress and entertainment. Philosophical ideas, famous trials, and great escapes highlight the drama and intrigue of human life. With so much to explore, this book ensures there is something to captivate every reader. Enjoy the journey!

Table of Contents

6.	Ancient Civilizations
8.	Unsolved Mysteries
10.	World Records
12.	Incredible Inventions
14.	Natural Phenomena
16.	Historical Events
18.	Famous Personalities
20.	Space Exploration
22.	Unusual Animals
24.	Mythology and Legends
26.	Hidden Places
28.	Rare Diseases
30.	Architectural Wonders
32.	Cultural Traditions
34.	Countries
36.	Languages
38.	Strange Laws
40.	Science Experiments
42.	Geographical Oddities
44.	Paranormal Activities
46.	Lost Cities
48.	Forgotten Technologies
50.	Human Body Facts
52.	Food and Drink
54.	Art and Literature
56.	Psychological Phenomena
58.	Extreme Sports
60.	Cryptozoology
62.	Time Travel Theories
64.	Famous Heists
66.	Linguistic Curiosities
68.	Historical Battles

70.	Notorious Pirates
72.	Inventive Hoaxes
74.	Space Mysteries
76.	Ancient Artifacts
78.	Superstitions
80.	Historical Figures' Secrets
82.	Exploration and Discovery
84.	Hidden Histories
86.	Medical Marvels
88.	Psychic Phenomena
90.	Rare Collectibles
92.	Artistic Techniques
94.	Global Festivals
96.	Military Innovations
98.	Technology Advancements
100.	Cinematic Trivia
102.	Philosophical Ideas
104.	Famous Trials
106.	Great Escapes
108.	Astronomical Events
110.	Fascinating Flora
112.	Haunted Locations
114.	Ancient Manuscripts
116.	Global Cuisines
118.	Urban Legends
120.	Historical Mysteries
122.	Social Movements
124.	Natural Disasters
126.	Literary Classics
128.	Art Forgery
130.	Historical Art Movements
132.	Modern Art
134.	Photographic Oddities
136.	Musical Instruments
138.	Famous Museums

140. Unique Hobbies
142. Animal Behavior
144. Marine Life
146. Aviation Facts
148. Astronomy
150. Ethnobotany
152. Political Intrigue
154. Global Conflicts
156. Espionage
158. Historical Buildings
160. Linguistic Evolution
162. Ethnomusicology
164. Meteorology
166. Epidemiology
168. Urban Planning
170. Material Science
172. Quantum Physics
174. Nanotechnology
176. Human Evolution
178. Forensic Science
180. Paleontology
182. Archaeological Finds
184. Conspiracy Theories
186. Historical Correspondence
188. Mythical Creatures
190. Lost Treasures
192. Unusual Professions
194. Remarkable Survivals
196. Historical Artifacts
198. Sports Trivia
200. Intellectual Property
202. Ethnography
204. Transhumanism
206. Dinosaurs

Ancient Civilizations

1. The Sumerians of Mesopotamia created the first known form of writing, cuneiform, around 3500 BCE.

2. The Indus Valley Civilization had sophisticated urban planning, including advanced drainage systems.

3. Ancient Egyptians believed in an afterlife and buried their pharaohs in elaborate tombs filled with treasures.

4. The Maya civilization developed a complex calendar system and were skilled astronomers.

5. The ancient city of Carthage was a major trade center in the Mediterranean before being destroyed by Rome in 146 BCE.

6. The Greeks held the first Olympic Games in 776 BCE to honor the god Zeus.

7. The ancient Chinese developed the concept of the Mandate of Heaven to justify the rule of their emperors.

8. The Roman Empire at its height spanned three continents: Europe, Africa, and Asia.

9. The Olmecs, known as the "mother culture" of Mesoamerica, created colossal stone heads weighing several tons.

10. The Persian Empire under Cyrus the Great was known for its policy of tolerance towards conquered peoples.

11. The Phoenicians, famous for their seafaring skills, created the first alphabet that influenced modern writing systems.

12. The Great Wall of China was built over several dynasties to protect against invasions from northern tribes.

13. The Akkadian Empire, established by Sargon of Akkad, was the first known empire in history.

14. The ancient Egyptians used a form of toothpaste made from powdered ashes, ox hooves, and burnt eggshells.

15. The Hittites were among the first to use iron weapons and chariots in warfare.

16. The Minoans of Crete are believed to have been the first Europeans to build paved roads.

17. The ancient city of Petra in Jordan was carved directly into the rock cliffs by the Nabataeans.

18. The Library of Alexandria in Egypt was one of the largest and most significant libraries of the ancient world.

19. The Inca Empire built an extensive network of roads and bridges across the Andes mountains.

20. The Etruscans of Italy greatly influenced Roman culture, including their architecture, religion, and art.

Unsolved Mysteries

1. The identity of Jack the Ripper, the infamous serial killer in 1888 London, remains unknown.

2. The disappearance of Malaysian Flight MH370 in 2014, with 239 people on board, remains unsolved.

3. The mystery of the Bermuda Triangle, where ships and planes have reportedly disappeared without a trace.

4. The Voynich Manuscript, a medieval book written in an unknown script, has never been deciphered.

5. The identity of the Somerton Man, found dead on an Australian beach in 1948, remains a mystery.

6. The disappearance of Amelia Earhart in 1937 during her attempt to circumnavigate the globe.

7. The true fate of the Romanovs, the Russian royal family executed in 1918, and the possibility of surviving members.

8. The location of the lost city of Atlantis, described by Plato, has never been confirmed.

9. The Oak Island Money Pit, believed to contain buried treasure, has confounded treasure hunters for centuries.

10. The cause of the Dyatlov Pass incident in 1959, where nine Russian hikers died under mysterious circumstances.

11. The identity of D.B. Cooper, who hijacked a plane in 1971 and parachuted away with ransom money, remains unknown.

12. The mystery of Stonehenge's construction and its true purpose.

13. The disappearance of the crew of the Mary Celeste, found adrift in the Atlantic in 1872.

14. The origin and purpose of the Nazca Lines in Peru, large geoglyphs etched into the desert floor.

15. The true identity of the Zodiac Killer, who terrorized California in the late 1960s and early 1970s.

16. The Tunguska event in 1908, a massive explosion in Siberia with no confirmed cause.

17. The fate of the Roanoke Colony, the first English settlement in America, which vanished without a trace.

18. The origin of the Wow! Signal, a strong radio signal detected by astronomers in 1977.

19. The death of American actress Natalie Wood in 1981, originally ruled accidental but still debated.

20. The mystery of the Green Children of Woolpit, who appeared in England in the 12th century speaking an unknown language.

World Records

1. The tallest man ever recorded was Robert Wadlow, who stood 8 feet 11 inches (2.72 meters) tall.

2. The heaviest man ever recorded was Jon Brower Minnoch, who weighed 1,400 pounds (635 kilograms).

3. The longest fingernails ever measured belonged to Lee Redmond, with a combined length of 28 feet (8.65 meters).

4. The longest recorded flight by a chicken is 13 seconds.

5. The longest continuous underwater breath-hold is 24 minutes and 3.45 seconds, achieved by Aleix Segura Vendrell.

6. The largest pizza ever made measured 13,580.28 square feet (1,261.65 square meters).

7. The fastest land speed recorded by a human is 27.8 mph (44.72 km/h), achieved by Usain Bolt.

8. The deepest dive by a human in a single breath is 214 meters (702 feet), achieved by Herbert Nitsch.

9. The oldest person ever verified was Jeanne Calment, who lived to be 122 years and 164 days old.

10. The longest marathon playing video games lasted 35 hours and 35 minutes.

11. The longest time spent in direct full-body contact with snow is 60 minutes, achieved by Oleksiy Gutsulyak.

12. The largest snowflake on record reportedly measured 15 inches wide and 8 inches thick.

13. The largest bubblegum bubble blown was 20 inches in diameter.

14. The longest time balancing on one foot is 76 hours and 40 minutes.

15. The most people making sand angels simultaneously is 1,387.

16. The longest time living with scorpions in a room is 33 days, achieved by Kanchana Ketkaew.

17. The most tattoos in 24 hours by a single person is 801.

18. The largest rubber band ball weighs 9,032 pounds (4,097 kilograms).

19. The tallest sandcastle ever built measured 57 feet and 11 inches (17.65 meters) tall.

20. The fastest marathon time while dressed as a fruit is 2 hours, 59 minutes, and 33 seconds.

Incredible Inventions

1. The wheel, invented around 3500 BCE in Mesopotamia, revolutionized transportation.

2. The printing press, invented by Johannes Gutenberg in 1440, made mass production of books possible.

3. The telephone, invented by Alexander Graham Bell in 1876, transformed global communication.

4. The light bulb, developed by Thomas Edison in 1879, brought electric lighting to homes and businesses.

5. The airplane, invented by the Wright brothers in 1903, revolutionized travel.

6. The internet, developed in the late 20th century, has changed the way we access and share information.

7. The steam engine, developed by James Watt in the 18th century, powered the Industrial Revolution.

8. The automobile, with Henry Ford's Model T in 1908, made personal transportation accessible to the masses.

9. The refrigerator, invented in 1834 by Jacob Perkins, transformed food preservation.

10. The computer, with early models like ENIAC in 1945, has revolutionized nearly every aspect of modern life.

11. The transistor, invented in 1947, is the building block of modern electronic devices.

12. The microwave oven, invented by Percy Spencer in 1945, revolutionized cooking.

13. The polio vaccine, developed by Jonas Salk in 1953, has saved millions of lives.

14. The artificial heart, with the first successful implant in 1982, has extended the lives of heart patients.

15. The GPS, developed by the U.S. Department of Defense in the 1970s, has transformed navigation.

16. The camera, with early models by Louis Daguerre in 1839, revolutionized how we capture memories.

17. The washing machine, with early electric models in the early 20th century, revolutionized household chores.

18. The solar panel, developed in the 1950s, has become a key technology in renewable energy.

19. The 3D printer, developed in the 1980s, is revolutionizing manufacturing and medical fields.

20. The electric car, with modern pioneers like Tesla, is transforming transportation and reducing carbon emissions.

Natural Phenomena

1. Aurora Borealis: The Northern Lights are caused by solar wind particles colliding with Earth's atmosphere.

2. Bioluminescence: Some marine organisms, like jellyfish and plankton, emit light through chemical reactions.

3. Tornadoes: The fastest wind speed ever recorded in a tornado was 318 mph in Moore, Oklahoma, in 1999.

4. Earthquakes: The most powerful earthquake ever recorded was a magnitude 9.5 in Chile in 1960.

5. Volcanic Eruptions: The eruption of Krakatoa in 1883 was so loud it was heard 3,000 miles away.

6. Lightning: A single bolt of lightning can contain up to 1 billion volts of electricity.

7. Hurricanes: Hurricane Patricia, which hit Mexico in 2015, had the highest wind speed ever recorded in a tropical cyclone at 215 mph.

8. Tsunamis: The 2004 Indian Ocean tsunami was caused by a 9.1-9.3 magnitude earthquake and killed over 230,000 people.

9. Sinkholes: The largest sinkhole, Xiaozhai Tiankeng in China, is over 2,100 feet deep and 1,760 feet wide.

10. Rainbows: A rainbow is a meteorological phenomenon caused by reflection, refraction, and dispersion of light in water droplets.

11. Hailstorms: The largest hailstone ever recorded in the U.S. was nearly 8 inches in diameter and fell in South Dakota in 2010.

12. Waterspouts: Waterspouts are tornadoes that form over water and can suck up fish, frogs, and other small aquatic animals.

13. Geysers: Old Faithful in Yellowstone National Park erupts approximately every 90 minutes, shooting water up to 185 feet in the air.

14. Dust Devils: These small, spinning vortices of dust and air can form on hot, sunny days in dry environments.

15. Ball Lightning: This rare phenomenon involves glowing, spherical objects that can last several seconds to minutes.

16. Supercells: These powerful thunderstorms can produce severe weather, including tornadoes, large hail, and strong winds.

17. Fire Whirls: Also known as fire tornadoes, these occur when intense heat and turbulent winds combine during wildfires.

18. Glaciers: The Lambert Glacier in Antarctica is the world's largest, stretching over 250 miles.

19. Monsoon: The Indian monsoon brings heavy rainfall and is vital for agriculture in the region.

20. Aurora Australis: The Southern Lights, similar to the Northern Lights, occur near the South Pole.

Historical Events

1. Fall of the Berlin Wall (1989): Marked the end of the Cold War and the beginning of German reunification.

2. Moon Landing (1969): Apollo 11, led by Neil Armstrong and Buzz Aldrin, marked humanity's first steps on the Moon.

3. American Revolution (1775-1783): Led to the independence of the United States from British rule.

4. French Revolution (1789-1799): Overthrew the monarchy and established a republic in France.

5. World War I (1914-1918): Involved many of the world's great powers and led to significant political changes in Europe.

6. World War II (1939-1945): The deadliest conflict in human history, leading to the downfall of Nazi Germany and Imperial Japan.

7. Industrial Revolution (1760-1840): Brought major changes in technology, industry, and society.

8. Signing of the Magna Carta (1215): Limited the powers of the English monarch and laid the foundation for modern democracy.

9. Discovery of America (1492): Christopher Columbus' voyage opened up the New World to European exploration and colonization.

10. The Renaissance (14th-17th Century): A cultural movement that profoundly affected European intellectual life.

11. Russian Revolution (1917): Led to the rise of the Soviet Union and the spread of communist ideology.

12. Fall of Constantinople (1453): Marked the end of the Byzantine Empire and the rise of the Ottoman Empire.

13. The Great Depression (1929): A severe worldwide economic depression that led to widespread poverty and unemployment.

14. Signing of the Declaration of Independence (1776): Proclaimed the thirteen American colonies as independent states.

15. The Reformation (1517): Initiated by Martin Luther, it led to major changes in the Christian Church.

16. The Black Death (1347-1351): Killed an estimated 25 million people in Europe, profoundly affecting society and economy.

17. The Space Race (1957-1969): A competition between the Soviet Union and the United States to achieve significant space exploration milestones.

18. The Printing Revolution (1440): The invention of the printing press by Gutenberg revolutionized the distribution of information.

19. The Atomic Bombings of Hiroshima and Nagasaki (1945): Led to Japan's surrender and the end of World War II.

20. The Fall of the Roman Empire (476 AD): Marked the end of ancient Rome and the beginning of the Middle Ages.

Famous Personalities

1. Albert Einstein: Developed the theory of relativity, significantly impacting modern physics.

2. Marie Curie: The first woman to win a Nobel Prize and the only person to win Nobel Prizes in two different sciences.

3. Leonardo da Vinci: Renaissance polymath known for his works in art, science, and engineering.

4. Mahatma Gandhi: Leader of the Indian independence movement against British rule through nonviolent resistance.

5. Martin Luther King Jr.: Civil rights leader who advocated for equality and justice through peaceful protest.

6. Cleopatra: The last active ruler of the Ptolemaic Kingdom of Egypt.

7. William Shakespeare: Widely regarded as one of the greatest playwrights and poets in the English language.

8. Nelson Mandela: Anti-apartheid revolutionary who became the first black president of South Africa.

9. Isaac Newton: Mathematician and physicist who formulated the laws of motion and universal gravitation.

10. Queen Elizabeth I: The Queen of England who led the country during the English Renaissance and defeated the Spanish Armada.

11. Winston Churchill: Prime Minister of the United Kingdom during World War II, known for his leadership and oratory.

12. Mozart: A prolific and influential composer of the Classical era.

13. Charles Darwin: Developed the theory of evolution by natural selection.

14. Mother Teresa: Catholic nun and missionary who dedicated her life to helping the poor in Calcutta, India.

15. Vincent van Gogh: Post-Impressionist painter known for his expressive and emotive works.

16. Galileo Galilei: Astronomer who played a major role in the Scientific Revolution.

17. Alexander the Great: King of Macedonia who created one of the largest empires in ancient history.

18. Pablo Picasso: A pioneering artist known for co-founding the Cubist movement.

19. Maya Angelou: Acclaimed poet, memoirist, and civil rights activist.

20. Steve Jobs: Co-founder of Apple Inc., revolutionized technology with products like the iPhone and the Macintosh.

Space Exploration

1. Sputnik 1 (1957): The first artificial Earth satellite launched by the Soviet Union.

2. Yuri Gagarin (1961): The first human to travel into space, orbiting the Earth.

3. Apollo 11 (1969): The first manned mission to land on the Moon, with Neil Armstrong and Buzz Aldrin.

4. Hubble Space Telescope (1990): Launched into low Earth orbit, providing unprecedented views of the universe.

5. Mars Rover Curiosity (2012): Landed on Mars to explore the planet's surface and geology.

6. International Space Station (1998): A habitable artificial satellite and research laboratory in low Earth orbit.

7. Voyager 1 (1977): The farthest human-made object from Earth, currently in interstellar space.

8. Challenger Disaster (1986): The Space Shuttle Challenger broke apart 73 seconds into its flight, leading to the deaths of its seven crew members.

9. Huygens Probe (2005): Landed on Saturn's moon Titan, providing detailed images and data.

10. SpaceX Dragon (2012): The first commercial spacecraft to deliver cargo to the ISS and return safely.

11. New Horizons (2015): The first mission to Pluto, providing detailed images and data of the dwarf planet.
12. Mars Insight (2018): A mission to study the interior of Mars and understand its seismic activity.

13. Juno (2011): A mission to study Jupiter's atmosphere, magnetic field, and structure.

14. Rosetta (2014): The first spacecraft to orbit a comet and deploy a lander, Philae, on its surface.

15. Kepler Space Telescope (2009): Discovered thousands of exoplanets, expanding our understanding of planetary systems.

16. Space Shuttle Program (1981-2011): Enabled frequent missions to space, including satellite deployment and ISS construction.

17. Pioneer 10 (1972): The first spacecraft to travel through the asteroid belt and make a flyby of Jupiter.

18. Galileo Orbiter (1995): Studied Jupiter and its moons, providing extensive data on the gas giant.

19. James Webb Space Telescope (2021): Designed to observe the most distant objects in the universe and study the formation of stars and planets.

20. Mars Sample Return Mission (Planned 2026): Aimed at collecting and returning samples from Mars to Earth for detailed analysis.

Unusual Animals

1. Axolotl: Also known as the Mexican walking fish, axolotls can regenerate entire limbs and even parts of their hearts and brains.

2. Aye-aye: This nocturnal lemur from Madagascar uses its long middle finger to tap on trees and locate insect larvae inside.

3. Blobfish: Found in deep waters off Australia, blobfish look like a gelatinous blob due to the lack of pressure at the ocean's surface.

4. Pangolin: Covered in scales made of keratin, pangolins are the only mammals with this unique feature.

5. Narwhal: Often called the "unicorn of the sea," narwhals have a long, spiral tusk that is actually an elongated tooth.

6. Leafy Sea Dragon: This marine creature resembles floating seaweed, providing excellent camouflage against predators.

7. Fossa: A carnivorous mammal from Madagascar, the fossa has retractable claws and a long tail for balance in trees.

8. Saiga Antelope: Native to the steppes of Eurasia, saiga antelopes have an unusual, bulbous nose that helps filter out dust.

9. Mantis Shrimp: Known for their powerful claws, mantis shrimp can punch with the speed of a bullet, capable of breaking glass.

10. Shoebill: This large, stork-like bird has a shoe-shaped bill used to catch and hold large fish.

11. Gerenuk: Also known as the giraffe gazelle, gerenuks can stand on their hind legs to reach leaves in tall bushes.

12. Star-Nosed Mole: This small mammal has a star-shaped nose with 22 fleshy appendages for detecting prey.

13. Tardigrade: Also known as water bears, tardigrades can survive extreme conditions, including the vacuum of space.

14. Okapi: The okapi is a relative of the giraffe but has zebra-like stripes on its legs.

15. Platypus: This egg-laying mammal has a duck bill, beaver tail, and otter feet, and males have venomous spurs.

16. Gobi Jerboa: A small rodent with disproportionately long hind legs, the jerboa moves by hopping.

17. Kakapo: A flightless parrot from New Zealand, the kakapo is nocturnal and critically endangered.

18. Marine Iguana: Found only on the Galápagos Islands, marine iguanas can swim and feed on algae underwater.

19. Thorny Devil: This Australian lizard has a spiky appearance and can change color to blend with its environment.

20. Anglerfish: Deep-sea anglerfish have a bioluminescent lure on their heads to attract prey in the dark ocean depths.

Mythology and Legends

1. Medusa: In Greek mythology, Medusa was a Gorgon with snakes for hair, and anyone who looked at her turned to stone.

2. Thor: Norse god of thunder, known for his mighty hammer Mjölnir, which could summon lightning.

3. Kraken: A legendary sea monster from Scandinavian folklore, said to dwell off the coast of Norway and Greenland.

4. Phoenix: A mythical bird that cyclically regenerates or is reborn, symbolizing immortality and renewal.

5. Minotaur: A creature with the body of a man and the head of a bull, imprisoned in the Labyrinth of Crete.

6. Banshee: In Irish folklore, a banshee is a spirit whose wail foretells the death of a family member.

7. Chupacabra: A legendary creature in Latin American folklore, said to attack livestock and drink their blood.

8. Anansi: A trickster spider god from West African folklore, known for his cunning and cleverness.

9. Leprechaun: A small, bearded fairy in Irish mythology, often depicted with a pot of gold at the end of the rainbow.

10. Basilisk: A legendary reptile said to cause death with a single glance, often depicted as a snake or serpent.

11. Fenrir: A monstrous wolf in Norse mythology, foretold to kill the god Odin during Ragnarok.

12. Yeti: Also known as the Abominable Snowman, a mythical ape-like creature said to inhabit the Himalayan mountains.

13. Quetzalcoatl: An Aztec god represented as a feathered serpent, associated with wind and learning.

14. Sirens: Mythical creatures in Greek mythology whose beautiful singing lured sailors to their doom.

15. Hercules: A Greek hero known for his incredible strength and his twelve labors, which included slaying the Hydra.

16. Loch Ness Monster: A legendary creature said to inhabit Loch Ness in Scotland, often depicted as a large, long-necked dinosaur-like creature.

17. Mermaids: Mythical sea creatures with the upper body of a human and the tail of a fish, appearing in various cultures worldwide.

18. Oni: Demonic creatures in Japanese folklore, often depicted with horns and terrifying appearances.

19. Valkyries: In Norse mythology, warrior maidens who chose those who would die and those who would live in battles.

20. Bigfoot: Also known as Sasquatch, a legendary ape-like creature said to inhabit the forests of North America.

Hidden Places

1. Machu Picchu: An ancient Incan city in Peru, hidden in the Andes mountains and rediscovered in 1911.

2. Petra: An archaeological city in Jordan, famous for its rock-cut architecture and water conduit system.

3. Angkor Wat: A massive temple complex in Cambodia, hidden in the jungle for centuries before its rediscovery.

4. Derinkuyu: An underground city in Turkey, capable of housing thousands of people and used for protection against invasions.

5. Antikythera Mechanism: An ancient Greek analog computer discovered in a shipwreck off the coast of Antikythera.

6. Mount Roraima: A tabletop mountain in South America, believed to be one of the oldest geological formations on Earth.

7. Cave of the Crystals: A cave in Mexico containing some of the largest natural crystals ever found.

8. Great Blue Hole: A giant marine sinkhole off the coast of Belize, known for its clear waters and diverse marine life.

9. Easter Island: Known for its mysterious moai statues, carved by the Rapa Nui people.

10. Baalbek: An ancient site in Lebanon, featuring some of the largest stone blocks used in construction.

11. Nazca Lines: Large geoglyphs in Peru, created by the Nazca culture and visible only from the air.

12. Lascaux Caves: A complex of caves in France famous for its Paleolithic cave paintings.

13. Socotra Island: An isolated island in Yemen, home to unique flora and fauna found nowhere else on Earth.

14. Mont Saint-Michel: A tidal island in France with a stunning medieval abbey.

15. Gobekli Tepe: An archaeological site in Turkey, considered the world's oldest known temple complex.

16. Salar de Uyuni: The world's largest salt flat in Bolivia, appearing as a vast, otherworldly landscape.

17. Pamukkale: Terraced hot springs in Turkey, known for their stunning white travertine formations.

18. Mogao Caves: A system of Buddhist cave temples in China, containing thousands of ancient manuscripts and artworks.

19. Bhangarh Fort: A historic fort in India, reputed to be one of the most haunted places in the country.

20. The Lost City of Z: A mythical city in the Amazon rainforest, sought by explorers like Percy Fawcett.

Rare Diseases

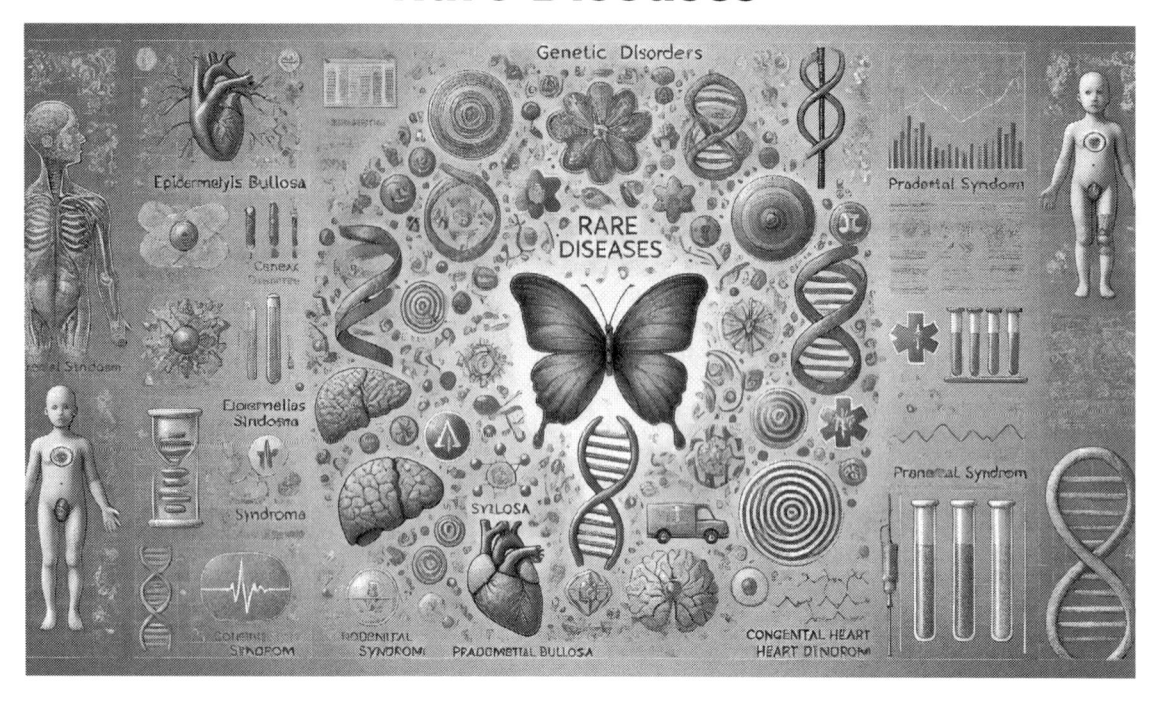

1. Progeria: A genetic disorder that causes children to age rapidly, often resulting in an early death.

2. Fibrodysplasia Ossificans Progressiva (FOP): A condition where soft tissues progressively turn into bone.

3. Hutchinson-Gilford Syndrome: Another name for Progeria, characterized by accelerated aging in children.

4. Morgellons Disease: A controversial condition where sufferers report fibers emerging from the skin.

5. Porphyria: A group of disorders caused by an accumulation of porphyrins, leading to skin and neurological problems.

6. Stiff Person Syndrome: A rare neurological disorder characterized by muscle stiffness and spasms.

7. Fatal Familial Insomnia: An inherited condition causing progressive insomnia, leading to hallucinations and death.

8. Kuru: A prion disease spread through cannibalism in Papua New Guinea, leading to tremors and fatal neurological decline.

9. Alice in Wonderland Syndrome: A condition causing distorted perception, where objects appear smaller or larger than they are.

10. Capgras Delusion: A psychiatric disorder where a person believes someone close to them has been replaced by an impostor.

11. Noma: A severe gangrenous infection affecting the face, primarily seen in malnourished children in developing countries.

12. Hyperthymesia: An extremely rare condition where individuals can recall an extraordinary amount of detail about their lives.

13. Fields' Disease: An extremely rare neuromuscular disease with only two known cases, affecting muscle control.

14. Moebius Syndrome: A rare neurological condition affecting facial muscle control, leading to facial paralysis.

15. Alien Hand Syndrome: A neurological disorder where one hand acts independently of the conscious mind.

16. Epidermodysplasia Verruciformis: Also known as tree man syndrome, a skin disorder leading to bark-like growths on the skin.

17. Aquagenic Urticaria: A condition where contact with water causes hives and severe skin reactions.

18. Paraneoplastic Pemphigus: A rare autoimmune blistering disorder associated with cancer.

19. Trimethylaminuria: A metabolic disorder causing the body to emit a strong, fishy odor.

20. Stoneman Syndrome: Another name for Fibrodysplasia Ossificans Progressiva (FOP), where muscles turn to bone over time.

Architectural Wonders

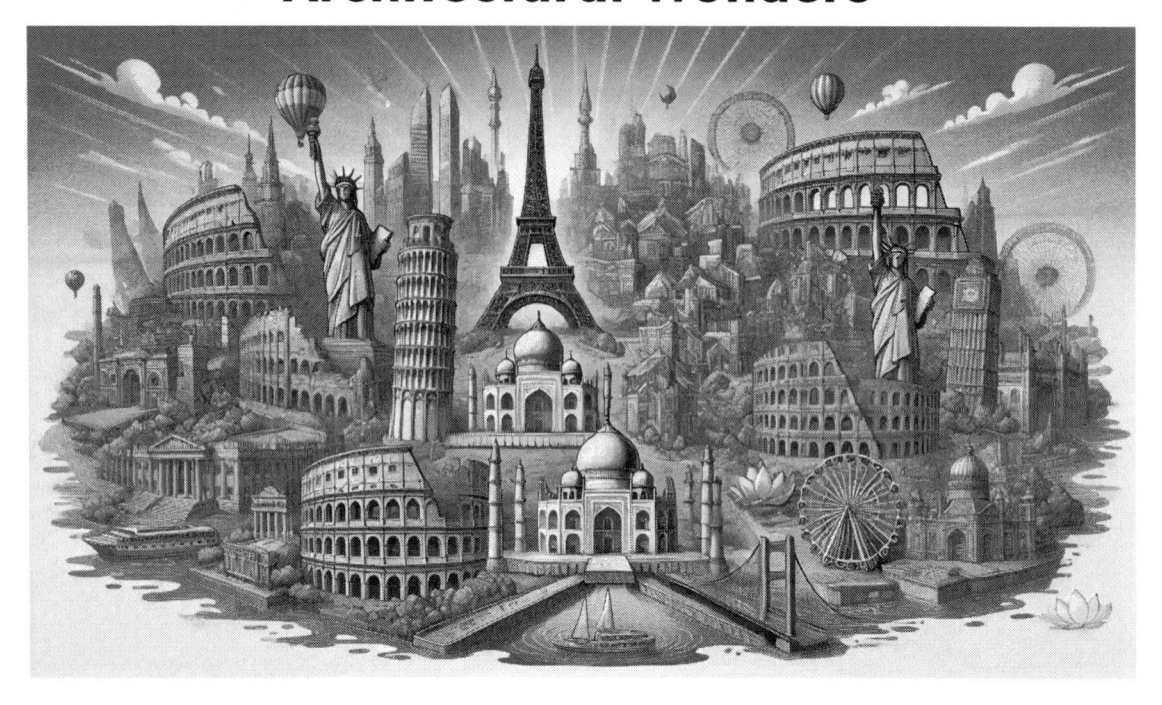

1. Great Wall of China: This massive wall stretches over 13,000 miles and was built to protect against invasions.

2. Taj Mahal: This stunning white marble mausoleum in India was built by Emperor Shah Jahan in memory of his wife Mumtaz Mahal.

3. Eiffel Tower: Constructed in 1889 for the Paris Exposition, it was the tallest man-made structure in the world until 1930.

4. Machu Picchu: An Incan city built in the 15th century, located high in the Andes Mountains of Peru.

5. Petra: The ancient city carved into red sandstone cliffs in Jordan is a UNESCO World Heritage site.

6. Colosseum: This large amphitheater in Rome was built in 70-80 AD and could hold up to 80,000 spectators.

7. Burj Khalifa: Located in Dubai, it is currently the tallest building in the world at 828 meters (2,717 feet).

8. Sagrada Familia: An unfinished basilica in Barcelona designed by Antoni Gaudí, construction began in 1882 and continues today.

9. Sydney Opera House: Known for its unique design, this iconic Australian building opened in 1973.

10. Pyramids of Giza: These ancient pyramids in Egypt, including the Great Pyramid, are among the Seven Wonders of the Ancient World.

11. Statue of Liberty: A symbol of freedom, this statue in New York Harbor was a gift from France to the United States in 1886.

12. Hagia Sophia: Originally built as a cathedral in Istanbul in 537 AD, it has served as a mosque and now a museum.

13. Golden Gate Bridge: An iconic suspension bridge in San Francisco, completed in 1937.

14. Angkor Wat: A vast temple complex in Cambodia, originally dedicated to the Hindu god Vishnu.

15. Neuschwanstein Castle: This fairy-tale castle in Germany was commissioned by King Ludwig II of Bavaria.

16. St. Basil's Cathedral: Known for its colorful onion domes, this cathedral is located in Moscow's Red Square.

17. Empire State Building: Completed in 1931, this Art Deco skyscraper in New York City was the tallest building in the world until 1970.

18. Pantheon: A former Roman temple, now a church, in Rome, known for its large dome and oculus.

19. Louvre Pyramid: The glass pyramid entrance to the Louvre Museum in Paris, designed by I.M. Pei.

20. Petronas Towers: Twin skyscrapers in Kuala Lumpur, Malaysia, once the tallest buildings in the world from 1998 to 2004.

Cultural Traditions

1. Day of the Dead (Día de los Muertos): A Mexican holiday honoring deceased loved ones with altars, food, and marigolds.

2. Chinese New Year: Celebrated with fireworks, dragon dances, and red envelopes containing money.

3. Diwali: The Hindu festival of lights, marking the victory of light over darkness.

4. Holi: An Indian festival of colors, celebrating the arrival of spring with vibrant powders and water fights.

5. Hanami: The Japanese tradition of viewing cherry blossoms in spring.

6. Oktoberfest: A German festival held in Munich, known for its beer tents, music, and traditional Bavarian clothing.

7. Thanksgiving: A North American holiday celebrating harvest and blessings, marked by a feast with turkey and other foods.

8. Carnival: A festive season before Lent, with parades, costumes, and dancing, most famously celebrated in Rio de Janeiro.

9. Eid al-Fitr: A Muslim festival marking the end of Ramadan, celebrated with feasts and giving to charity.

10. Lunar New Year: Celebrated in various Asian countries, marking the start of the lunar calendar year.

11. La Tomatina: A Spanish festival in Buñol where participants throw tomatoes at each other.

12. Mardi Gras: Celebrated in New Orleans with parades, masks, and beads, marking the beginning of Lent.

13. Bastille Day: France's national day on July 14th, commemorating the French Revolution with fireworks and parades.

14. Inti Raymi: An Incan festival in Peru celebrating the sun god Inti.

15. Yule: A traditional Germanic winter festival, now associated with Christmas celebrations.

16. Tet: The Vietnamese New Year, celebrated with family gatherings and traditional foods.

17. Sinterklaas: A Dutch tradition where Saint Nicholas delivers gifts to children on December 5th.

18. Songkran: The Thai New Year, celebrated with water fights and cleansing rituals.

19. Up Helly Aa: A Viking fire festival in Scotland's Shetland Islands, involving torchlight processions and burning a Viking ship.

20. Mid-Autumn Festival: Celebrated in East Asia with mooncakes and lanterns, honoring the moon and harvest.

Countries

1. China has the largest population in the world, with over 1.4 billion people.

2. Vatican City is the smallest country in the world by both area and population.

3. Russia is the largest country in the world by land area.

4. Canada has the longest coastline of any country in the world.

5. Australia is the only country that is also a continent.

6. Japan consists of 6,852 islands.

7. Brazil has the largest population of Catholics in the world.

8. Iceland is the only country in the world without mosquitoes.

9. France is the most visited country in the world.

10. Libya is mostly covered by the Sahara Desert, making it one of the driest countries in the world.

11. Saudi Arabia is the largest country in the world without a river.

12. Mongolia has the lowest population density of any country in the world.

13. Singapore is one of the only three city-states in the world, along with Monaco and Vatican City.

14. Finland has been ranked as the happiest country in the world multiple times.

15. Norway is home to the world's longest road tunnel, the Laerdal Tunnel.

16. Chile has the world's driest desert, the Atacama Desert.

17. Ethiopia is the only country in Africa never to have been colonized, apart from a brief Italian occupation.

18. New Zealand was the first country to grant women the right to vote in 1893.

19. India has the largest postal network in the world, with over 1.5 lakh post offices.

20. South Africa has three capital cities: Pretoria, Bloemfontein, and Cape Town.

Languages

1. Mandarin Chinese is the most spoken language in the world.

2. English is the most widely studied second language in the world.

3. Spanish is the second most spoken native language in the world.

4. French is the official language of 29 countries, making it the second most widely spoken official language.

5. Arabic is written from right to left, unlike most other languages.

6. Hindi is written in the Devanagari script.

7. Russian uses the Cyrillic alphabet.

8. Japanese uses three writing systems: Kanji, Hiragana, and Katakana.

9. Portuguese is the official language of nine countries.

10. Bengali is the seventh most spoken language in the world.

11. Punjabi is the 10th most spoken language in the world.

12. German is the most widely spoken native language in Europe.

13. Korean uses a unique writing system called Hangul.

14. Italian is a Romance language, derived from Latin.

15. Swahili is widely spoken in East Africa and has many Arabic loanwords.

16. Greek has the longest documented history of any Indo-European language.

17. Hebrew was revived as a spoken language in the 19th and 20th centuries.

18. Thai is known for its complex tonal system.

19. Icelandic has changed very little since the Viking era.

20. Esperanto is a constructed language created to foster international communication.

Strange Laws

1. Chewing Gum Ban in Singapore: It's illegal to import and sell chewing gum, except for medical reasons.

2. No High Heels at Historical Sites in Greece: To protect ancient monuments, wearing high heels is prohibited.

3. No Frowning in Pocatello, Idaho: A law from the 1940s states that it's illegal not to smile in public.

4. No Flushing the Toilet After 10 PM in Switzerland: In some apartment buildings, it's considered noise pollution.

5. No Feeding Pigeons in Venice, Italy: To protect historical sites and reduce the pigeon population.

6. No Public Displays of Affection in Dubai: Holding hands, hugging, and kissing in public can lead to fines or imprisonment.

7. No Reincarnation Without Permission in China: Tibetan monks must seek government approval to reincarnate.

8. No Slicing a Potato in Germany: According to an old law, you cannot cut a potato in half and place it on a fence post.

9. No Wearing Masks in Public in Denmark: To prevent criminal activity and ensure identification.

10. No Camouflage Clothing in the Caribbean: Several Caribbean countries ban civilians from wearing camouflage.

11. No Using a Black Car on Sundays in Denver, Colorado: An old law prohibited black cars from being on the roads on Sundays.

12. No Collecting Rainwater in Colorado: It was illegal to collect rainwater in barrels until the law changed in 2016.

13. No Biting Your Neighbor's Pumpkin in Ottumwa, Iowa: A local ordinance makes it illegal to bite into another person's pumpkin.

14. No Pinching in Portugal: It's illegal to pinch someone in Portugal, punishable by fines.

15. No Humming in Public on Sundays in Michigan: A law prohibits public humming on Sundays.

16. No Chewing Bread and Chicken Together in Massachusetts: An old law states you can't eat bread and chicken simultaneously in the streets.

17. No Flying Kites in Victoria, Australia: It's illegal to fly a kite in a public place if it bothers others.

18. No Wearing Lacy Underwear in Russia: A regulation bans the sale of lace underwear due to health concerns.

19. No Dying Without a Funeral Plan in Sarpourenx, France: It's illegal to die without owning a burial plot in this village.

20. No Ice Cream on Cherry Pie in Kansas: An old law prohibits serving ice cream on cherry pie in Kansas.

Science Experiments

1. Double-Slit Experiment: Demonstrated the wave-particle duality of light and matter.

2. Cavendish Experiment: Measured the force of gravitational attraction between masses and determined the density of Earth.

3. Miller-Urey Experiment: Simulated early Earth conditions and produced organic compounds, showing potential origins of life.

4. Michelson-Morley Experiment: Demonstrated the absence of the luminiferous aether, leading to the theory of special relativity.

5. Pavlov's Dogs: Ivan Pavlov's experiment demonstrated classical conditioning with dogs salivating at the sound of a bell.

6. Stanford Prison Experiment: Examined the psychological effects of perceived power, with participants role-playing as guards and prisoners.

7. Galileo's Leaning Tower of Pisa Experiment: Demonstrated that objects fall at the same rate regardless of mass.

8. Rutherford Gold Foil Experiment: Discovered the nucleus of the atom by observing the deflection of alpha particles.

9. Rosalind Franklin's X-ray Diffraction: Provided crucial evidence of the double helix structure of DNA.

10. Hershey-Chase Experiment: Confirmed that DNA is the genetic material in viruses.

11. Feynman's Double-Slit Experiment with Electrons: Showed that electrons exhibit both particle and wave behavior.

12. Asch Conformity Experiments: Studied the extent to which social pressure influences conformity in individuals.

13. Hawthorne Effect: Showed that individuals modify their behavior in response to being observed.

14. Watson and Crick's DNA Model: Built the first accurate model of DNA's double helix structure.

15. Stanley Milgram's Obedience Experiment: Examined the extent to which individuals obey authority figures, even against their conscience.

16. Loftus and Palmer's Car Crash Study: Investigated the effects of language on memory recall.

17. LIGO Experiment: Detected gravitational waves, confirming a prediction of Einstein's general relativity.

18. Dolly the Sheep: The first mammal cloned from an adult somatic cell, demonstrating the feasibility of cloning.

19. Large Hadron Collider: The world's largest particle accelerator, used to discover the Higgs boson particle.

20. Hubble Space Telescope: Provided unprecedented views of the universe, leading to numerous astronomical discoveries.

Geographical Oddities

1. Mount Roraima: This tabletop mountain in South America serves as a triple border point for Venezuela, Brazil, and Guyana.

2. Lake Baikal: Located in Siberia, it's the world's deepest and oldest freshwater lake, containing about 20% of the world's unfrozen freshwater.

3. The Dead Sea: At 430.5 meters below sea level, it is the Earth's lowest elevation on land and has extremely high salinity.

4. The Bermuda Triangle: An area in the North Atlantic Ocean where numerous ships and airplanes have disappeared under mysterious circumstances.

5. Marble Caves: Located in Chile, these strikingly beautiful caves are formed in pure marble and surrounded by turquoise water.

6. Salar de Uyuni: The world's largest salt flat, located in Bolivia, which becomes a giant mirror during the rainy season.

7. Socotra Island: An island in Yemen with unique flora and fauna, including the dragon's blood tree, which looks like an umbrella.

8. Devil's Tower: A monolithic igneous formation in Wyoming, famous for its unique hexagonal columns.

9. Giant's Causeway: A coastal area in Northern Ireland featuring about 40,000 interlocking basalt columns, the result of an ancient volcanic fissure eruption.

10. Pamukkale: Known for its white travertine terraces and thermal waters, located in Turkey.

11. Eye of the Sahara: Also known as the Richat Structure, this circular formation in Mauritania is visible from space.

12. Darvaza Gas Crater: Often called the "Door to Hell," this natural gas field in Turkmenistan has been burning since 1971.

13. Danakil Depression: One of the hottest places on Earth, located in Ethiopia, known for its alien-like landscape.

14. Chocolate Hills: A geological formation in the Philippines made up of at least 1,260 hills that turn brown in the dry season.

15. Red Beach: Located in China, this beach gets its name from the red-colored seaweed that thrives in its saline-alkali soil.

16. Lake Hillier: A bright pink lake in Australia, whose color is thought to be due to the presence of certain algae and bacteria.

17. Antelope Canyon: A slot canyon in Arizona known for its wave-like structure and light beams shining down into the openings.

18. Great Blue Hole: A giant marine sinkhole off the coast of Belize, popular for scuba diving.

19. Blood Falls: An outflow of iron oxide-tainted saltwater flowing from the Taylor Glacier in Antarctica.

20. Banaue Rice Terraces: 2,000-year-old terraces in the Philippines, carved into the mountains by the Ifugao people.

Paranormal Activities

1. The Amityville Horror: A series of events in a house in Amityville, New York, where a family claimed to experience terrifying paranormal phenomena.

2. The Bell Witch: A poltergeist legend from Tennessee, involving a spirit that tormented the Bell family in the early 19th century.

3. The Enfield Poltergeist: A famous case of supposed poltergeist activity in London during the late 1970s.

4. The Winchester Mystery House: A mansion in California built by Sarah Winchester, supposedly haunted by the ghosts of those killed by Winchester rifles.

5. The Stanley Hotel: Inspiration for Stephen King's "The Shining," this Colorado hotel is reputedly haunted.

6. The Bermuda Triangle: An area in the North Atlantic Ocean associated with numerous unexplained disappearances of ships and airplanes.

7. Loch Ness Monster: A legendary creature said to inhabit Loch Ness in Scotland, often depicted as a large, long-necked aquatic dinosaur.

8. Area 51: A highly secretive U.S. military base in Nevada, rumored to be the site of UFO sightings and alien autopsies.

9. The Myrtles Plantation: A plantation in Louisiana reputed to be one of America's most haunted homes.

10. The Tower of London: Known for its dark history and numerous ghost sightings, including Anne Boleyn.

11. Borley Rectory: Dubbed the "most haunted house in England," known for ghostly apparitions and poltergeist activity.

12. Aokigahara Forest: Also known as the Suicide Forest in Japan, it is believed to be haunted by the spirits of those who have died there.

13. Eastern State Penitentiary: An abandoned prison in Philadelphia, known for reports of ghostly activity.

14. The Whaley House: A historic house in San Diego, California, often cited as one of the most haunted places in America.

15. Poveglia Island: An island in Italy, used as a quarantine station for plague victims and later as a mental asylum, rumored to be haunted.

16. The Brown Lady of Raynham Hall: A famous ghost photograph taken in Raynham Hall, England, depicting a spectral figure descending a staircase.

17. The Jersey Devil: A legendary creature said to inhabit the Pine Barrens of New Jersey.

18. The Mothman: A mysterious creature reported in Point Pleasant, West Virginia, associated with the collapse of the Silver Bridge in 1967.

19. The Queen Mary: A retired ocean liner docked in Long Beach, California, reputed to be haunted by multiple spirits.

20. Edinburgh Vaults: Underground chambers in Edinburgh, Scotland, known for ghostly sightings and paranormal investigations.

Lost Cities

1. Atlantis: A legendary island first mentioned by Plato, said to have sunk into the ocean.

2. El Dorado: A mythical city of gold believed to be located in South America.

3. Pompeii: An ancient Roman city buried by the eruption of Mount Vesuvius in 79 AD.

4. Machu Picchu: An Incan city in Peru, rediscovered by Hiram Bingham in 1911.

5. Petra: An ancient city in Jordan, rediscovered in the 19th century, known for its rock-cut architecture.

6. Troy: An ancient city in present-day Turkey, made famous by Homer's epic poems.

7. Angkor: A capital city of the Khmer Empire in Cambodia, home to Angkor Wat.

8. Teotihuacan: An ancient Mesoamerican city in Mexico, known for its large pyramids.

9. Mesa Verde: Cliff dwellings built by the Ancestral Puebloans in Colorado, USA.

10. Vijayanagara: A powerful South Indian city, now in ruins in Karnataka, India.

11. Palmyra: An ancient Semitic city in Syria, once a vital trading center.

12. Nan Madol: A ruined city built on a series of artificial islets in Micronesia.

13. Cahokia: A pre-Columbian Native American city near present-day St. Louis, Missouri.

14. Heracleion: An ancient Egyptian city submerged off the coast of Alexandria.

15. Mohenjo-Daro: An Indus Valley civilization city in present-day Pakistan.

16. Great Zimbabwe: A medieval city in southeastern Zimbabwe, known for its large stone structures.

17. Tikal: An ancient Mayan city in present-day Guatemala.

18. Leptis Magna: A prominent city of the Roman Empire, located in present-day Libya.

19. Ubar: Also known as the "Atlantis of the Sands," a legendary lost city in the Arabian Peninsula.

20. Hattusa: The capital of the Hittite Empire, located in modern Turkey.

Forgotten Technologies

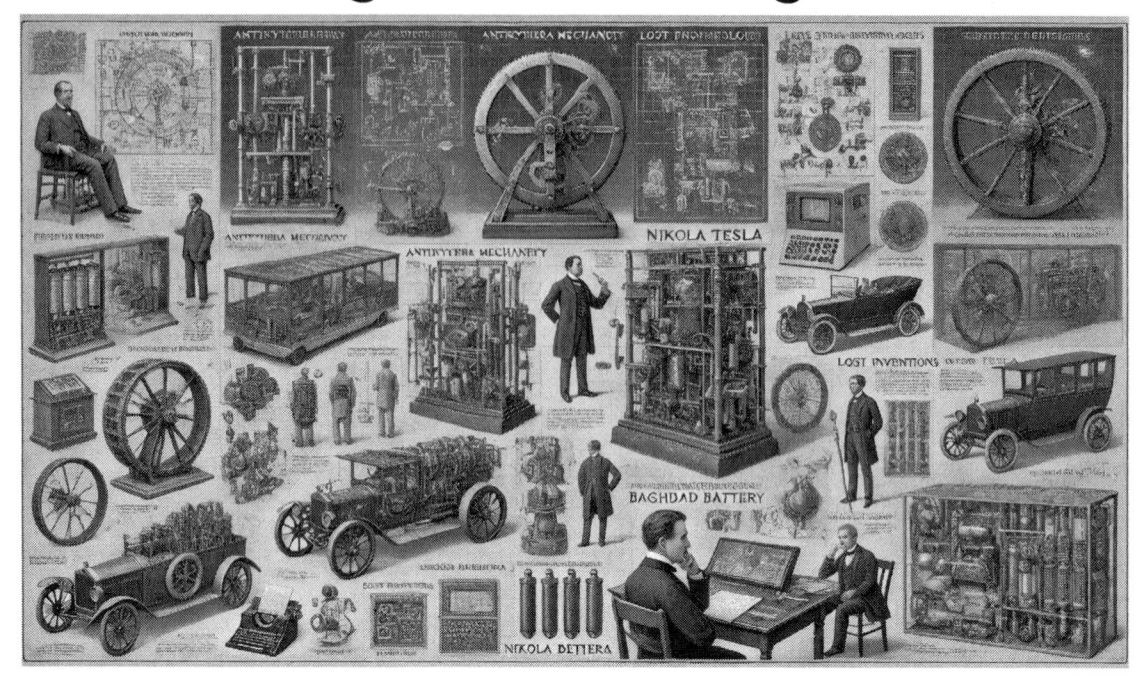

1. Antikythera Mechanism: An ancient Greek analog computer used to predict astronomical positions and eclipses.

2. Roman Concrete: A durable building material used by ancient Romans, its exact composition and longevity surpass modern concrete.

3. Damascus Steel: A type of steel used in the Middle Ages, renowned for its strength and ability to hold a sharp edge.

4. Greek Fire: An incendiary weapon used by the Byzantine Empire, capable of burning even on water.

5. Baghdad Battery: An ancient artifact some believe to be an early form of battery.

6. Flexible Glass: Allegedly invented in ancient Rome but destroyed by Emperor Tiberius, fearing it would devalue gold and silver.

7. Lost Wax Casting: An ancient method for making intricate metal objects, still not fully replicated in its original form.

8. Peruvian Rope Bridges: Constructed using braided grass, these suspension bridges were remarkably strong and durable.

9. Incan Stone Masonry: The precise stone-cutting technique used to build structures like Machu Picchu without mortar.

10. Vitrum Flexile: A legendary unbreakable glass supposedly invented during the Roman Empire.

11. Aeolipile: An early steam engine described by Hero of Alexandria, used to demonstrate the principles of steam power.

12. Stradivarius Violins: Violins made by Antonio Stradivari, known for their exceptional sound quality, the secret of which is still not fully understood.

13. Tesla's Wireless Power Transmission: Nikola Tesla's experiments aimed to transmit electricity wirelessly over long distances.

14. Roman Aqueducts: Ingenious engineering systems used to transport water over long distances using gravity.

15. Pyramid Construction Techniques: The methods used by ancient Egyptians to construct the pyramids remain a topic of debate and mystery.

16. Philosopher's Stone: A mythical substance in alchemy believed to turn base metals into gold and grant immortality.

17. Ancient Greek Automata: Early mechanical devices created by inventors like Hero of Alexandria, capable of performing complex movements.

18. Mithridatium: An antidote for poison reputedly used by King Mithridates VI, the exact composition of which is unknown.

19. Roman Hypocaust: An ancient Roman system of underfloor heating.

20. Nabataean Water Management: Advanced techniques used by the Nabataeans to manage and conserve water in the desert city of Petra.

Human Body Facts

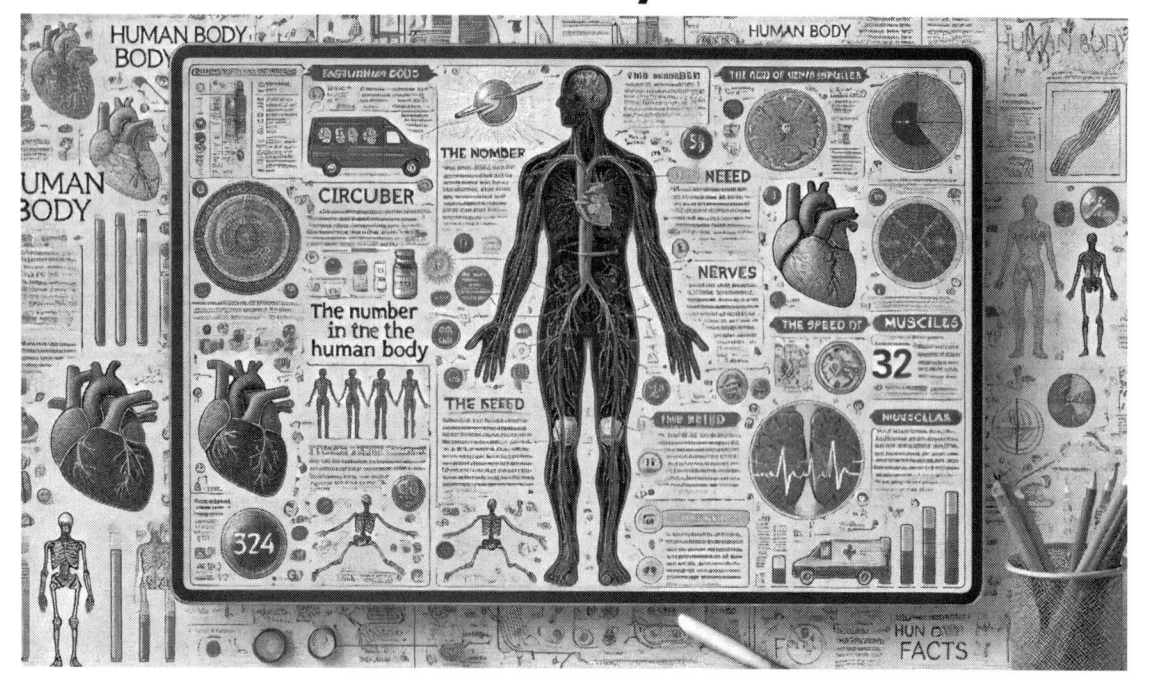

1. Number of Cells: The human body is composed of around 37.2 trillion cells.

2. Bones: At birth, humans have around 270 bones, which fuse to become 206 bones by adulthood.

3. Skin: The skin is the body's largest organ, covering an average of 22 square feet.

4. Heart: The human heart beats approximately 100,000 times a day.

5. Blood Vessels: If laid end to end, the blood vessels in the human body would stretch over 60,000 miles.

6. Brain: The human brain contains about 86 billion neurons.

7. Muscles: There are over 600 muscles in the human body.

8. DNA: If the DNA in all your cells were stretched out, it would reach the sun and back over 600 times.

9. Taste Buds: The average human tongue has around 10,000 taste buds.

10. Regeneration: The human liver can regenerate itself from as little as 25% of its tissue.

11. Sweat: Humans have between 2 to 4 million sweat glands, and women generally have more than men.

12. Blinking: The average person blinks about 15-20 times per minute.

13. Saliva: A human produces about 1-2 liters of saliva each day.

14. Teeth: Enamel, the outer layer of teeth, is the hardest substance in the human body.

15. Hair: On average, a person has around 100,000 to 150,000 hair follicles on their scalp.

16. Blood Cells: The body produces about 2 million red blood cells every second.

17. Sensory Receptors: The fingertips have about 2,500 touch receptors per square centimeter.

18. Immune System: The average adult has about 1.2 gallons of blood circulating in their body.

19. Synapses: The brain can form new connections or synapses, which is the basis of learning and memory.

20. Lung Capacity: An average person's lungs can hold about 6 liters of air.

Food and Drink

1. Chocolate: Theobromine in chocolate can be toxic to dogs and cats.

2. Honey: Honey is the only food that does not spoil; edible honey has been found in ancient Egyptian tombs.

3. Caviar: True caviar comes from the sturgeon fish and can cost up to $10,000 per kilogram.

4. Pizza: The Margherita pizza was named after Queen Margherita of Savoy in 1889.

5. Apples: There are over 7,500 varieties of apples grown worldwide.

6. Coffee: Coffee is the second most traded commodity in the world after oil.

7. Bananas: Bananas are berries, but strawberries are not.

8. Spices: Saffron is the most expensive spice in the world, often costing over $500 per ounce.

9. Peanut Butter: It takes about 540 peanuts to make a 12-ounce jar of peanut butter.

10. Wine: The oldest known winery was discovered in Armenia and dates back to about 4100 BC.

11. Cheese: The world produces more than 21 million metric tons of cheese annually.

12. Pasta: There are over 600 different shapes of pasta.

13. Tea: Tea is the most consumed beverage in the world after water.

14. Bread: The oldest evidence of bread-making dates back 14,000 years, found in Jordan.

15. Tomatoes: Tomatoes were once considered poisonous in Europe.

16. Garlic: One clove of garlic contains 5 milligrams of calcium, 12 milligrams of potassium, and over 100 sulfuric compounds.

17. Avocado: Avocados are technically berries.

18. Beer: Beer is one of the oldest beverages produced by humans, dating back to at least the 5th millennium BC.

19. Maple Syrup: It takes about 40 gallons of sap to produce one gallon of maple syrup.

20. Coconut Water: Coconut water can be used as a substitute for blood plasma in emergencies.

Art and Literature

1. Mona Lisa: Leonardo da Vinci's Mona Lisa is one of the most recognized and valuable paintings in the world.

2. Shakespeare: William Shakespeare coined many English phrases still in use today, such as "break the ice" and "wild-goose chase."

3. The Thinker: Auguste Rodin's The Thinker was originally part of a larger work called The Gates of Hell.

4. Van Gogh: Vincent van Gogh only sold one painting during his lifetime, The Red Vineyard.

5. First Novel: The Tale of Genji, written by Murasaki Shikibu in the early 11th century, is often considered the world's first novel.

6. Literature Prize: The Nobel Prize in Literature was first awarded in 1901 to Sully Prudhomme.

7. The Starry Night: Vincent van Gogh painted The Starry Night while in a mental asylum in Saint-Rémy-de-Provence.

8. Dante's Inferno: Dante Alighieri's Divine Comedy, which includes Inferno, is a cornerstone of Italian literature.

9. Harry Potter: J.K. Rowling's Harry Potter series has sold over 500 million copies worldwide.

10. Cubism: Pablo Picasso and Georges Braque developed Cubism, a revolutionary style of modern art.

11. Gutenberg Bible: Printed in the 1450s, the Gutenberg Bible was the first major book printed using movable type.

12. The Scream: Edvard Munch's The Scream is one of the most iconic images in art history.

13. Jane Austen: Jane Austen published her novels anonymously; her works became widely popular after her death.

14. Michelangelo: Michelangelo painted the Sistine Chapel ceiling between 1508 and 1512.

15. Surrealism: Salvador Dalí was a prominent figure in the Surrealist movement, known for his dreamlike and bizarre imagery.

16. Beowulf: An Old English epic poem, Beowulf is one of the most important works of Anglo-Saxon literature.

17. Guernica: Pablo Picasso's Guernica depicts the horrors of war and is considered one of the most powerful anti-war paintings.

18. The Odyssey: Attributed to Homer, The Odyssey is an epic poem that follows the adventures of Odysseus.

19. Impressionism: Claude Monet's Impression, Sunrise gave the name to the Impressionist movement.

20. Mark Twain: Samuel Clemens, known by his pen name Mark Twain, wrote classics like The Adventures of Tom Sawyer and Adventures of Huckleberry Finn.

Psychological Phenomena

1. Cognitive Dissonance: The mental discomfort experienced when holding two or more contradictory beliefs or values.

2. Placebo Effect: A beneficial effect produced by a placebo drug or treatment, due to the patient's belief in the treatment.

3. Déjà Vu: The feeling that one has lived through the present situation before.

4. Barnum Effect: The tendency to accept vague or general statements as personally meaningful.

5. Confirmation Bias: The tendency to search for, interpret, and remember information that confirms one's preconceptions.

6. Pareidolia: The tendency to perceive familiar patterns, such as faces, in random stimuli.

7. Phantom Limb: The sensation that an amputated or missing limb is still attached to the body and moving.

8. Prosopagnosia: Also known as face blindness, a condition where individuals cannot recognize faces.

9. Stockholm Syndrome: A condition where hostages develop a psychological alliance with their captors during captivity.

10. False Memory: A psychological phenomenon where a person recalls something that did not happen.

11. Synesthesia: A condition where one sensory experience is involuntarily linked to another, such as seeing colors when hearing music.

12. Inattentional Blindness: The failure to notice a fully visible but unexpected object because attention was engaged on another task.

13. The Baader-Meinhof Phenomenon: The illusion in which something that has recently come to one's attention suddenly seems to appear frequently.

14. Learned Helplessness: A condition in which a person suffers from a sense of powerlessness, arising from a traumatic event or persistent failure.

15. Bystander Effect: The tendency for individuals to be less likely to help a victim when other people are present.

16. Halo Effect: The tendency to let an overall impression of a person influence judgments about their specific traits.

17. Social Loafing: The phenomenon where individuals exert less effort when working in a group compared to working alone.

18. Fundamental Attribution Error: The tendency to attribute others' behaviors to their character while attributing our own behaviors to our circumstances.

19. Hindsight Bias: The inclination to see events as having been predictable after they have already occurred.

20. Pygmalion Effect: The phenomenon where higher expectations lead to an increase in performance.

Extreme Sports

1. BASE Jumping: BASE stands for Building, Antenna, Span, and Earth – the fixed objects from which participants jump.

2. Wingsuit Flying: This sport involves gliding through the air in a special jumpsuit with fabric between the legs and arms.

3. Big Wave Surfing: Surfers ride waves at least 20 feet high, with spots like Maui's Jaws and Portugal's Nazaré being famous locations.

4. Free Solo Climbing: Climbing without ropes or safety gear, famously practiced by Alex Honnold on El Capitan.

5. Cave Diving: Exploring underwater caves, considered one of the most dangerous diving activities due to the risks of entrapment and decompression sickness.

6. Freestyle Motocross: Riders perform acrobatic stunts while airborne on motocross bikes.

7. Skydiving: Jumping from an aircraft and free-falling before deploying a parachute.

8. Ice Climbing: Climbing frozen waterfalls or ice-covered rock faces using specialized gear like ice axes and crampons.

9. Downhill Mountain Biking: Racing down steep and rough terrain, often involving jumps and technical obstacles.

10. Bungee Jumping: Leaping from a height with an elastic cord attached to the ankles, pioneered by the Oxford University Dangerous Sports Club in 1979.

11. Kite Surfing: Combining aspects of wakeboarding, windsurfing, and paragliding, riders use a large controllable kite to pull themselves across water.

12. Parkour: A training discipline where practitioners move rapidly through an area, typically urban, using techniques like running, jumping, and climbing.

13. Whitewater Rafting: Navigating rivers with varying degrees of rough water in an inflatable raft.

14. Volcano Boarding: Sliding down the slopes of a volcano on a board, popular on Nicaragua's Cerro Negro.

15. Extreme Skiing: Skiing down steep, often dangerous slopes with difficult terrain, like cliffs and narrow chutes.

16. Slacklining: Balancing and walking on a narrow, flexible webbing tensioned between two anchor points.

17. Freediving: Diving underwater without breathing apparatus, aiming for depth, distance, or time.

18. Ultramarathons: Races longer than the traditional marathon distance of 26.2 miles, sometimes exceeding 100 miles.

19. Wingsuit Base Jumping: Combining wingsuit flying and BASE jumping, where participants glide before deploying a parachute.

20. Sandboarding: Riding down sand dunes on a board, similar to snowboarding but on sand.

Cryptozoology

1. Bigfoot: Also known as Sasquatch, reported sightings mainly in the Pacific Northwest of North America.

2. Loch Ness Monster: A large aquatic creature said to inhabit Scotland's Loch Ness.

3. Chupacabra: A creature said to attack livestock, particularly goats, and drink their blood, first reported in Puerto Rico.

4. Yeti: An ape-like creature reported in the Himalayan mountains, also known as the Abominable Snowman.

5. Mothman: A large, winged humanoid reportedly seen in Point Pleasant, West Virginia, in the 1960s.

6. Jersey Devil: A creature from New Jersey folklore, described as a flying biped with hooves.

7. Kraken: A legendary sea monster said to dwell off the coasts of Norway and Greenland.

8. Thunderbird: A giant bird-like creature from Native American legends, reported sightings mainly in North America.

9. Mermaids: Mythical sea creatures with the upper body of a human and the tail of a fish, reported in various cultures worldwide.

10. Mokele-Mbembe: A dinosaur-like creature said to inhabit the Congo River basin in Africa.

11. Ogopogo: A lake monster reported to inhabit Okanagan Lake in British Columbia, Canada.

12. Dover Demon: A small, humanoid creature reported in Dover, Massachusetts, in 1977.

13. Bunyip: A mythical creature from Aboriginal Australian folklore, said to inhabit swamps and billabongs.

14. Flatwoods Monster: A humanoid entity reported in Flatwoods, West Virginia, in 1952, described with glowing eyes and a pointed head.

15. Lizard Man: A reptilian humanoid reported in South Carolina, said to have clawed feet and hands.

16. Beast of Bray Road: A werewolf-like creature reported in Wisconsin, described as a bipedal wolf.

17. Ahool: A giant bat-like creature reported in Java, Indonesia.

18. Globster: An unidentified organic mass washed up on a beach, often mistaken for a sea monster.

19. Ropen: A flying creature from Papua New Guinea, described as a large bat with a glowing light.

20. Fouke Monster: A Bigfoot-like creature reported in Fouke, Arkansas, made famous by the 1972 film "The Legend of Boggy Creek."

Time Travel Theories

1. Einstein's Theory of Relativity: Suggests that time dilation occurs when approaching the speed of light, where time slows down for the traveler.

2. Wormholes: Hypothetical passages through space-time that could create shortcuts for long journeys across the universe.

3. Cosmic Strings: Theoretical one-dimensional defects in space-time, which could allow time travel if they exist.

4. Tipler Cylinder: A hypothetical massive, rotating cylinder proposed by Frank Tipler that could enable time travel through its rotation.

5. Alcubierre Drive: A theoretical concept involving a warp drive that could allow faster-than-light travel, potentially enabling time travel.

6. Time Loops: A concept where time can repeat itself in a loop, creating the possibility of experiencing the same events multiple times.

7. Multiverse Theory: Suggests that parallel universes exist, and time travel could involve moving between these different realities.

8. Grandfather Paradox: A time travel paradox where changing the past could negate the time traveler's existence, such as killing one's grandfather before one's parent is born.

9. Novikov Self-Consistency Principle: States that any actions taken by a time traveler were always part of history, preventing paradoxes.

10. Time Slip: A phenomenon where individuals claim to have temporarily experienced a different time period.

11. Causality Violation: The idea that time travel could violate the cause-and-effect relationship, leading to potential paradoxes.

12. Quantum Tunneling: A concept in quantum mechanics where particles can pass through barriers, potentially allowing for time travel on a microscopic scale.

13. Retrocausality: The idea that future events can affect the past, allowing for information or objects to travel backward in time.

14. Hawking's Chronology Protection Conjecture: Suggests that the laws of physics prevent time travel to avoid paradoxes.

15. Tachyons: Hypothetical particles that travel faster than light, which could theoretically move backward in time.

16. Closed Timelike Curves: Paths in space-time that return to the same point in space and time, theoretically allowing for time travel.

17. Gödel's Rotating Universe: A solution to Einstein's field equations proposed by Kurt Gödel, suggesting a rotating universe could allow for time travel.

18. Time Crystals: Hypothetical structures that repeat in time, potentially allowing for time manipulation.

19. Block Universe Theory: Suggests that past, present, and future exist simultaneously in a four-dimensional space-time block.

20. Temporal Displacement: The idea of moving an object or person to a different point in time without traversing the intervening time.

Famous Heists

1. Great Train Robbery (1963): A gang of 15 men stole £2.6 million from a Royal Mail train in England.

2. Lufthansa Heist (1978): Thieves stole around $5 million in cash and $875,000 in jewelry from JFK Airport, as depicted in the movie "Goodfellas."

3. Isabella Stewart Gardner Museum Heist (1990): Thieves stole 13 pieces of art valued at around $500 million, including works by Vermeer and Rembrandt.

4. Brinks Job (1950): Thieves stole $2.7 million from the Brink's Armored Car Depot in Boston, known as the "crime of the century."

5. Antwerp Diamond Heist (2003): Thieves stole over $100 million worth of diamonds from a vault in the Antwerp Diamond Center.

6. D.B. Cooper Hijacking (1971): A man hijacked a plane, extorted $200,000, and parachuted away, never to be seen again.

7. Banco Central Heist (2005): Thieves tunneled into the Banco Central in Fortaleza, Brazil, stealing about $70 million.

8. Hatton Garden Heist (2015): A group of elderly men broke into a safe deposit company in London, stealing an estimated £14 million.

9. Knightsbridge Security Deposit Heist (1987): Thieves stole an estimated $98 million from a security deposit box in London.

10. United California Bank Burglary (1972): Thieves stole $9 million in cash and valuables from a bank in Laguna Niguel, California.

11. Central Bank of Iraq Heist (2003): Saddam Hussein allegedly ordered the theft of $1 billion from the Central Bank of Iraq.

12. Securitas Depot Robbery (2006): Thieves stole £53 million from a cash depot in Tonbridge, England.

13. Great Maple Syrup Heist (2012): Thieves stole 3,000 tons of syrup valued at $18 million from a warehouse in Quebec, Canada.

14. Banco Rio Heist (2006): Thieves in Argentina stole $20 million from a bank by taking hostages and escaping through a tunnel.

15. Crown Jewels Theft (1671): Colonel Thomas Blood attempted to steal the Crown Jewels from the Tower of London but was captured.

16. Carlton Hotel Heist (1994): Thieves stole $60 million worth of jewelry from the Carlton Hotel in Cannes, France.

17. Millennium Dome Raid (2000): Thieves attempted to steal diamonds worth £350 million but were foiled by the police.

18. Graff Diamonds Robbery (2009): Thieves stole £40 million worth of jewelry from a Graff Diamonds store in London.

19. Banco de Brasilia Heist (2010): Thieves tunneled into the bank and stole around $7 million.

20. Harry Winston Heist (2008): Thieves stole $108 million worth of jewelry from the Harry Winston store in Paris.

Linguistic Curiosities

1. Longest Word: The longest word in the English language, according to the Oxford English Dictionary, is "pneumonoultramicroscopicsilicovolcanoconiosis."

2. Language Families: There are about 7,000 languages spoken in the world today, grouped into roughly 140 language families.

3. Pirahã Language: Spoken by an indigenous people in Brazil, it has no fixed words for numbers or specific colors.

4. Tone Languages: In tonal languages like Mandarin, the meaning of a word can change based on the pitch or tone used.

5. Clicks: Some African languages, such as Xhosa and Zulu, use click sounds as consonants.

6. Alphabet: The Hawaiian alphabet has only 13 letters: 5 vowels and 8 consonants.

7. Etymology: The word "etymology" itself comes from the Greek word "etymon," meaning "true sense."

8. Polysynthetic Languages: Languages like Inuktitut and Navajo can express complex ideas with a single word.

9. Endangered Languages: It's estimated that one language dies every two weeks, with many at risk of extinction.

10. Sign Languages: American Sign Language (ASL) is different from British Sign Language (BSL); they are not mutually intelligible.

11. Invented Languages: Esperanto is a constructed international auxiliary language created by L. L. Zamenhof in 1887.

12. Palindrome: A word, phrase, number, or other sequences of characters that reads the same forward and backward, such as "racecar."

13. Longest Place Name: The full name of a hill in New Zealand is Taumatawhakatangihangakoauauotamateaturipukakapikimaunga horonukupokaiwhenuakitanatahu.

14. Isolating Languages: Languages like Vietnamese and Mandarin have very few or no inflections for grammar.

15. Gendered Nouns: In languages like German, nouns have genders that are not necessarily related to the gender of the objects.

16. Verb-Initial Languages: In languages like Hawaiian and Welsh, sentences often start with verbs.

17. Whistling Languages: Silbo Gomero, used in the Canary Islands, is a whistled form of Spanish.

18. Pangrams: Sentences that include every letter of the alphabet at least once, like "The quick brown fox jumps over the lazy dog."

19. Hanzi Characters: Chinese has over 50,000 characters, but about 3,000 are needed to read a newspaper.

20. Loanwords: English has borrowed words from many languages, such as "bungalow" from Hindi and "ballet" from French.

Historical Battles

1. Battle of Marathon (490 BC): A pivotal battle in which the Greeks defeated the Persians, marking the first victory of the Greeks in the Persian Wars.

2. Battle of Thermopylae (480 BC): Famous for the stand of 300 Spartans against the much larger Persian army.

3. Battle of Gaugamela (331 BC): Alexander the Great's decisive victory over Darius III of Persia.

4. Battle of Hastings (1066): William the Conqueror defeated King Harold II to become the king of England.

5. Battle of Agincourt (1415): A major English victory in the Hundred Years' War, noted for the effectiveness of the English longbow.

6. Siege of Constantinople (1453): The Ottoman Empire captured Constantinople, marking the end of the Byzantine Empire.

7. Spanish Armada (1588): The English navy defeated the Spanish Armada, marking the rise of England as a naval power.

8. Battle of Blenheim (1704): A key battle in the War of the Spanish Succession where the Duke of Marlborough led the Allies to victory.

9. Battle of Saratoga (1777): Turning point in the American Revolutionary War, leading to French support for the Americans.

10. Battle of Trafalgar (1805): Admiral Nelson's decisive naval victory over the French and Spanish fleets.

11. Battle of Waterloo (1815): The final defeat of Napoleon Bonaparte by the British and Prussian forces.

12. Battle of Antietam (1862): The bloodiest single-day battle in American history during the Civil War.

13. Battle of Gettysburg (1863): A turning point in the American Civil War, resulting in a Union victory.

14. Battle of the Somme (1916): One of the largest battles of World War I, notable for its high casualties.

15. Battle of Midway (1942): A decisive naval battle in the Pacific Theater of World War II, leading to a significant victory for the Allies.

16. D-Day (1944): The Allied invasion of Normandy during World War II, marking the beginning of the end for Nazi Germany.

17. Battle of Stalingrad (1942-1943): A brutal battle in World War II, ending with the Soviet Union's victory over Nazi Germany.

18. Battle of Tours (732): Charles Martel defeated the Umayyad Caliphate, halting the Muslim advance into Western Europe.

19. Battle of Lepanto (1571): A naval engagement where the Holy League defeated the Ottoman fleet.

20. Battle of Kadesh (1274 BC): An ancient battle between the Egyptians under Ramesses II and the Hittites, one of the earliest battles with detailed accounts.

Notorious Pirates

1. Blackbeard (Edward Teach): One of the most famous pirates of the Golden Age of Piracy, known for his fearsome appearance.

2. Captain Kidd (William Kidd): Initially hired to hunt pirates, he turned to piracy himself and was eventually executed.

3. Anne Bonny: A notorious female pirate who, along with Mary Read, sailed with "Calico Jack" Rackham.

4. Mary Read: An English pirate who fought alongside Anne Bonny and was known for her disguise as a man.

5. Bartholomew Roberts (Black Bart): Captured over 400 ships during his career, making him one of the most successful pirates.

6. Calico Jack (John Rackham): Known for his distinctive clothing and for sailing with female pirates Anne Bonny and Mary Read.

7. Henry Morgan: A Welsh privateer who became the Lieutenant Governor of Jamaica.

8. Sir Francis Drake: An English sea captain and privateer who circumnavigated the globe and raided Spanish ships.

9. Charles Vane: Known for his cruelty and refusal to accept the King's pardon, he was eventually captured and executed.

10. Edward Low: Infamous for his brutality, he was feared for his torture of prisoners.

11. Stede Bonnet: Known as the "Gentleman Pirate," he was a wealthy landowner who turned to piracy.

12. Black Sam Bellamy: Known as the "Prince of Pirates," he was one of the wealthiest pirates in recorded history.

13. Benjamin Hornigold: A pirate and privateer who later turned pirate hunter, capturing his former comrades.

14. Henry Every: Known for his capture of the Mughal ship Ganj-i-Sawai, making him one of the richest pirates.

15. Jean Lafitte: A French pirate and privateer who operated in the Gulf of Mexico.

16. Thomas Tew: An English pirate known for his voyages to the Indian Ocean and the Red Sea.

17. Israel Hands: A close associate of Blackbeard who was given command of one of his ships.

18. Christopher Condent: A pirate who raided the Indian Ocean and later accepted a pardon, becoming a plantation owner.

19. Francois l'Olonnais: A French buccaneer known for his ruthless attacks on Spanish ships and settlements.

20. John Hawkins: An English slave trader and privateer who conducted several profitable voyages to the West Indies.

Inventive Hoaxes

1. Piltdown Man: In 1912, Charles Dawson claimed to have found the "missing link" between ape and man, but it was later revealed as a forgery.

2. Crop Circles: Complex patterns in crops that were initially thought to be made by aliens, but many were later admitted to be man-made.

3. War of the Worlds Broadcast (1938): Orson Welles' radio adaptation caused panic as listeners believed a real Martian invasion was occurring.

4. The Turk: An 18th-century chess-playing automaton that was revealed to have a human operator inside.

5. Cardiff Giant: A petrified giant "discovered" in 1869, later revealed to be a hoax by George Hull.

6. The Cottingley Fairies: Photographs taken by two girls in 1917 claimed to show real fairies, later admitted to be paper cutouts.

7. The Great Moon Hoax: In 1835, the New York Sun published articles claiming astronomers had discovered life on the Moon.

8. Hitler Diaries: Supposed diaries of Adolf Hitler, published in 1983, were later proven to be forgeries.

9. Loch Ness Monster: The famous 1934 "surgeon's photograph" was revealed to be a hoax using a toy submarine.

10. Fiji Mermaid: A sideshow exhibit presented by P.T. Barnum in the 1840s, it was actually a monkey's torso sewn to a fish tail.

11. Paul Is Dead: A conspiracy theory that claimed Paul McCartney died in 1966 and was replaced by a look-alike.

12. Lovenstein Institute IQ Report: A satirical report falsely claimed to measure the IQ of U.S. presidents.

13. The Cottingley Fairies: The photographs taken by two young girls, later admitted to be a prank using paper cutouts.

14. Alien Autopsy: A 1995 film purported to show a government autopsy of an alien, later admitted to be staged.

15. Sokal Affair: Physicist Alan Sokal submitted a nonsensical paper to a cultural studies journal to show how jargon could mask absurdity.

16. Bigfoot Film: The 1967 Patterson-Gimlin film purporting to show Bigfoot has been widely debated and often considered a hoax.

17. Dihydrogen Monoxide Hoax: A parody of scientific reporting that highlights the chemical dangers of water by using a technical name.

18. Spaghetti Tree Hoax: A 1957 BBC April Fool's Day segment showed Swiss farmers harvesting spaghetti from trees.

19. The Madagascar Plan: A Nazi proposal to relocate Jews to Madagascar, later revealed as propaganda.

20. The Ghostwatch Hoax: A 1992 British TV mockumentary that caused panic as viewers believed a live ghost investigation was real.

Space Mysteries

1. Dark Matter: An unseen form of matter that makes up about 27% of the universe's mass-energy content.

2. Dark Energy: A mysterious force causing the acceleration of the universe's expansion.

3. The Great Attractor: A gravitational anomaly in intergalactic space that pulls galaxies toward it.

4. Fast Radio Bursts (FRBs): Millisecond-long bursts of radio waves from distant galaxies, origin unknown.

5. The Pioneer Anomaly: Unexpected deviations in the trajectories of the Pioneer 10 and Pioneer 11 spacecraft.

6. Tabby's Star: A star with irregular dimming, speculated to be caused by an alien megastructure or dust clouds.

7. The Wow! Signal: A strong narrowband radio signal detected in 1977, possibly of extraterrestrial origin.

8. Oumuamua: The first known interstellar object passing through the Solar System, with unknown origins.

9. Kuiper Cliff: A sudden drop-off in the number of objects in the Kuiper Belt beyond 50 AU from the Sun.

10. Galactic Center Radio Transients: Mysterious radio signals from the center of the Milky Way.

11. The Hubble Constant: Discrepancies in the measured rate of the universe's expansion.

12. The Missing Baryon Problem: A significant amount of ordinary matter predicted by models remains undetected.

13. The Fermi Paradox: The apparent contradiction between the high probability of extraterrestrial life and the lack of evidence.

14. Gamma-Ray Bursts (GRBs): Extremely energetic explosions observed in distant galaxies, origins still debated.

15. Black Hole Information Paradox: The question of what happens to information that falls into a black hole.

16. The Cold Spot: An unusually large and cold area in the Cosmic Microwave Background radiation.

17. Quasars: Extremely bright and distant objects powered by supermassive black holes.

18. The Edge of the Universe: The question of what, if anything, lies beyond the observable universe.

19. Cosmic Rays: High-energy particles from outer space, with unknown origins for the highest energy ones.

20. The Age of the Universe: Discrepancies between different methods of measuring the universe's age.

Ancient Artifacts

1. Rosetta Stone: A granodiorite stele inscribed with a decree in three scripts, key to deciphering Egyptian hieroglyphs.

2. Dead Sea Scrolls: Ancient Jewish manuscripts found in the Qumran Caves, including texts from the Hebrew Bible.

3. Terracotta Army: Thousands of life-sized clay soldiers buried with China's first emperor, Qin Shi Huang.

4. Pyramids of Giza: Monumental tombs in Egypt built for the pharaohs during the Old Kingdom.

5. Tutankhamun's Mask: The gold funerary mask of the young Egyptian pharaoh, discovered in his intact tomb.

6. Antikythera Mechanism: An ancient Greek analog computer used to predict astronomical positions and eclipses.

7. Stonehenge: A prehistoric monument in England, consisting of a ring of standing stones.

8. Machu Picchu: An Incan citadel set high in the Andes Mountains in Peru.

9. Sphinx of Giza: A limestone statue of a reclining sphinx, a mythical creature, near the Great Pyramid.

10. Easter Island Moai: Monolithic human figures carved by the Rapa Nui people on Easter Island.

11. Venus of Willendorf: A statuette of a female figure, estimated to be around 30,000 years old.

12. The Parthenon: A temple on the Athenian Acropolis dedicated to the goddess Athena.

13. Cuneiform Tablets: Ancient writing on clay tablets from Mesopotamia, one of the earliest forms of writing.

14. Nazca Lines: Large geoglyphs made in the soil of the Nazca Desert in southern Peru.

15. Shroud of Turin: A linen cloth bearing the image of a man, believed by some to be the burial shroud of Jesus.

16. Royal Tombs of Ur: Burial sites of Sumerian royalty, containing elaborate grave goods.

17. Lascaux Cave Paintings: Prehistoric cave paintings found in southwestern France, estimated to be around 17,000 years old.

18. Olmec Colossal Heads: Seventeen basalt heads sculpted by the Olmec civilization of ancient Mesoamerica.

19. Celtic Crosses: Stone crosses found in Ireland and Britain, often richly decorated with knotwork.

20. Baghdad Battery: A set of three artifacts found together: a ceramic pot, a tube of copper, and a rod of iron, hypothesized to be an ancient battery.

Superstitions

1. Black Cats: In many cultures, black cats are considered bad luck, though in some, they are seen as good luck.

2. Walking Under a Ladder: Believed to bring bad luck due to the shape of the ladder forming a triangle, representing the Holy Trinity.

3. Breaking a Mirror: Said to bring seven years of bad luck, originating from the belief that mirrors hold a piece of the soul.

4. Knocking on Wood: Done to ward off bad luck, originating from ancient beliefs in tree spirits.

5. Friday the 13th: Considered an unlucky day in Western superstition, possibly due to the combination of an unlucky number and day.

6. Throwing Salt Over Your Shoulder: Thought to ward off bad luck or evil spirits after spilling salt.

7. Four-Leaf Clovers: Considered a symbol of good luck due to their rarity.

8. Opening an Umbrella Indoors: Believed to bring bad luck, possibly due to its association with ancient sun gods.

9. Itchy Palm: In some cultures, an itchy right palm means you'll receive money, while an itchy left palm means you'll lose money.

10. Horseshoes: Hanging a horseshoe over a door is believed to bring good luck and protection.

11. Rabbit's Foot: Carried as a good luck charm, believed to bring protection and prosperity.

12. Spilling Salt: Considered bad luck, possibly originating from its high value in ancient times.

13. Broken Clock: Some believe that a stopped or broken clock is a bad omen.

14. Bird in the House: A bird flying into the house is often seen as an omen of death.

15. Crossing Fingers: Done to wish for good luck or to protect oneself from bad luck.

16. Lucky Penny: Finding a penny, especially heads-up, is considered good luck.

17. Wishbone: Two people pulling apart a dried wishbone can make a wish; the one with the larger piece will have their wish granted.

18. Red String: In some cultures, wearing a red string is believed to ward off evil spirits or bad luck.

19. Dream Catchers: Originating from Native American culture, they are believed to filter out bad dreams and allow only good dreams to pass through.

20. Sweeping Feet: Sweeping the floor and accidentally sweeping over someone's feet is believed to bring bad luck, such as never getting married.

Historical Figures' Secrets

1. Thomas Jefferson: Kept a long-term relationship with his slave Sally Hemings and had several children with her.

2. Albert Einstein: Had an illegitimate daughter, Lieserl, with his first wife, Mileva Maric, who disappeared from records after 1903.

3. Winston Churchill: Suffered from depression, which he referred to as his "black dog."

4. Queen Elizabeth I: Known as the "Virgin Queen," there were rumors about her romantic relationships with Robert Dudley and others.

5. George Washington: Had false teeth made from various materials, including human teeth, animal teeth, and ivory, but not wood.

6. Napoleon Bonaparte: Was not actually short; he was around 5'7", average height for his time. The misconception came from a difference in French and British measurement units.

7. Edgar Allan Poe: Married his 13-year-old cousin, Virginia Clemm, when he was 27.

8. Catherine the Great: Rumored to have died in bizarre circumstances, but she actually died of a stroke.

9. John F. Kennedy: Suffered from Addison's disease, a serious adrenal insufficiency, which was kept secret during his presidency.

10. Isaac Newton: Was deeply interested in alchemy and the occult, which was not widely known during his lifetime.

11. Abraham Lincoln: Suffered from depression and had several breakdowns during his life.

12. Vincent van Gogh: Only sold one painting during his lifetime, "The Red Vineyard."

13. Florence Nightingale: Had a lifelong chronic illness thought to be brucellosis, which she kept secret while working.

14. Ludwig van Beethoven: Wrote some of his greatest works while being completely deaf.

15. Rasputin: Was highly influential in the Russian court due to his alleged healing abilities, which kept the Tsar's son alive.

16. Franz Kafka: Ordered his friend Max Brod to burn all his unpublished manuscripts after his death, a wish Brod ignored.

17. Cleopatra: Was actually of Greek descent, being a member of the Ptolemaic dynasty, which ruled Egypt.

18. Marie Antoinette: Did not actually say "Let them eat cake"; it was a rumor spread to incite anger against her.

19. Fidel Castro: Survived over 600 assassination attempts during his life.

20. Ernest Hemingway: Worked as a spy for the U.S. during World War II, using his boat to patrol for German submarines.

Exploration and Discovery

1. Christopher Columbus: Discovered the New World in 1492, although he believed he had found a new route to India.

2. Marco Polo: Traveled to China and served at the court of Kublai Khan, documenting his journeys in "The Travels of Marco Polo."

3. Ferdinand Magellan: Led the first expedition to circumnavigate the globe, though he was killed in the Philippines before completing the journey.

4. Vasco da Gama: The first person to sail directly from Europe to India, opening up a new trade route.

5. James Cook: Made detailed maps of Newfoundland and the Pacific, including the first European contact with Australia and Hawaii.

6. Lewis and Clark: Led an expedition to explore the American West, providing valuable information about the region.

7. Roald Amundsen: First to reach the South Pole in 1911.

8. Hernán Cortés: Conquered the Aztec Empire in present-day Mexico.

9. Zheng He: Chinese explorer who led seven voyages during the Ming Dynasty, reaching as far as Africa.

10. David Livingstone: Explored Africa and sought the source of the Nile River.

11. Jacques Cartier: Claimed Canada for France and explored the Saint Lawrence River.

12. Sir Francis Drake: The first Englishman to circumnavigate the globe.

13. Henry Hudson: Explored present-day New York and Canada, searching for the Northwest Passage.

14. Bartolomeu Dias: First European to sail around the southern tip of Africa, opening the sea route to Asia.

15. John Cabot: Discovered parts of North America under the commission of Henry VII of England.

16. Alexander von Humboldt: Explored Latin America, contributing significantly to the fields of geography and natural sciences.

17. Ibn Battuta: Moroccan explorer who traveled extensively throughout the Islamic world and beyond in the 14th century.

18. Ernest Shackleton: Led expeditions to Antarctica, known for the heroic rescue of his crew from the stranded ship Endurance.

19. Thor Heyerdahl: Sailed the Kon-Tiki raft from South America to the Polynesian islands to prove ancient peoples could have made long sea voyages.

20. Howard Carter: Discovered the tomb of Tutankhamun in 1922, one of the most significant archaeological finds.

Hidden Histories

1. The Lost Colony of Roanoke: The first English settlement in America that mysteriously disappeared, leaving only the word "Croatoan" carved into a tree.

2. Cahokia: A large pre-Columbian Native American city near present-day St. Louis that had complex urban planning and a large population.

3. Doggerland: An area now submerged beneath the North Sea that once connected Great Britain to mainland Europe.

4. The Kingdom of Kush: An ancient African kingdom located in present-day Sudan, known for its pyramids and rivalry with Egypt.

5. Timbuktu: Once a thriving center of trade and learning in West Africa, now mostly forgotten.

6. Göbekli Tepe: An archaeological site in Turkey that predates Stonehenge by 6,000 years and challenges our understanding of early civilization.

7. The Etruscans: An ancient civilization in Italy that significantly influenced Roman culture but whose language and origins remain a mystery.

8. The Indus Valley Civilization: One of the world's earliest urban cultures, with sophisticated city planning and advanced technology, yet much about it remains unknown.

9. The Olmecs: The first major civilization in Mexico, known for their colossal head sculptures and mysterious influence on later cultures.

10. The Anasazi: An ancient Native American culture in the southwestern United States, known for their cliff dwellings and sudden disappearance.

11. The Sea Peoples: A confederation of naval raiders who attacked ancient Mediterranean civilizations around 1200 BCE, their origins and fate remain unclear.

12. The Voynich Manuscript: An illustrated codex written in an unknown script and language, its purpose and origin are still debated.

13. Vinland: A region of North America explored by Norse Vikings, as recorded in the sagas of Leif Erikson.

14. Catalhoyuk: An ancient city in Turkey, one of the oldest known, featuring early examples of urban living and art.

15. Mohenjo-Daro: An advanced city of the Indus Valley Civilization with sophisticated architecture and urban planning.

16. The Scythians: Nomadic warriors from Central Asia, known for their skills in horseback riding and archery, influencing many cultures.

17. The Hittites: An ancient Anatolian people who built a vast empire and clashed with Egypt at the Battle of Kadesh.

18. The Nubian Kingdoms: Ancient African kingdoms along the Nile, known for their powerful rulers and rich culture.

19. The Minoans: An advanced civilization on the island of Crete, known for their palaces and extensive trade networks.

20. The Khmer Empire: A powerful empire in Southeast Asia, known for building Angkor Wat and other monumental temples.

Medical Marvels

1. Penicillin: Discovered by Alexander Fleming in 1928, it was the first true antibiotic and has saved countless lives.

2. Insulin: Discovered by Frederick Banting and Charles Best in 1921, it revolutionized the treatment of diabetes.

3. X-rays: Discovered by Wilhelm Conrad Roentgen in 1895, they allow doctors to see inside the body without surgery.

4. Vaccination: Edward Jenner developed the first successful smallpox vaccine in 1796.

5. DNA Structure: Discovered by James Watson and Francis Crick in 1953, it paved the way for genetic research.

6. Organ Transplants: The first successful human kidney transplant was performed in 1954 by Joseph Murray.

7. MRI: Magnetic resonance imaging, developed in the 1970s, revolutionized medical diagnostics.

8. Polio Vaccine: Developed by Jonas Salk in 1955, it significantly reduced the incidence of polio worldwide.

9. Anesthesia: First successfully used in surgery by William Morton in 1846, it transformed surgical procedures.

10. Heart Transplant: The first successful human heart transplant was performed by Christiaan Barnard in 1967.

11. Antiretroviral Therapy: Developed in the 1990s, it transformed HIV from a fatal disease into a manageable condition.

12. Artificial Heart: The first successful implantation of a total artificial heart was performed in 1982 by Barney Clark.

13. Stem Cell Therapy: First used successfully in the 1980s, it holds promise for treating a range of diseases.

14. CRISPR: A revolutionary gene-editing technology that allows for precise changes to DNA.

15. Bionic Limbs: Advanced prosthetics that can be controlled by the user's nerves and muscles.

16. Cochlear Implants: Devices that provide a sense of sound to individuals who are profoundly deaf or severely hard of hearing.

17. In Vitro Fertilization (IVF): First successfully used in 1978, it has helped millions of couples conceive.

18. Immunotherapy: A breakthrough cancer treatment that uses the body's immune system to fight cancer cells.

19. Telemedicine: The use of telecommunication technology to provide clinical health care from a distance, especially crucial during the COVID-19 pandemic.

20. Genome Sequencing: The ability to sequence an individual's genome has opened up new possibilities in personalized medicine and disease prevention.

Psychic Phenomena

1. Telepathy: The ability to transmit thoughts or feelings between individuals without using any known human sensory channels.

2. Clairvoyance: The supposed ability to gain information about an object, person, location, or physical event through extrasensory perception.

3. Precognition: The ability to perceive or predict future events before they happen.

4. Psychokinesis: The purported ability to move or manipulate objects with the mind alone.

5. Mediumship: The practice of mediating communication between spirits of the dead and living human beings.

6. Remote Viewing: The practice of seeking impressions about a distant or unseen target using extrasensory perception.

7. Astral Projection: An out-of-body experience where a person's consciousness is said to leave the physical body and travel in an astral plane.

8. Aura Reading: The ability to perceive the energy field surrounding a person, often visualized as a colorful aura.

9. Dowsing: A type of divination used to locate ground water, buried metals, gemstones, or other objects, often using a dowsing rod.

10. Automatic Writing: Writing produced without conscious thought, often attributed to the influence of spirits.

11. Psychometry: The ability to obtain information about a person or event by touching an object related to them.

12. Dream Telepathy: The supposed ability to communicate with others through dreams.

13. Retrocognition: The ability to perceive or describe events from the past.

14. Energy Healing: Techniques like Reiki that claim to use the practitioner's energy to heal another person.

15. Spoon Bending: The ability to bend metal objects like spoons using psychic powers.

16. ESP (Extrasensory Perception): The ability to receive information beyond the known physical senses.

17. Crystal Gazing: The practice of looking into a crystal ball to predict future events or gain hidden knowledge.

18. Tarot Reading: Using tarot cards to gain insights into past, present, and future events through a spread of cards.

19. Runes: Ancient alphabetic symbols used for divination and magical purposes.

20. Pendulum Divination: Using a pendulum to answer questions or locate objects through its swinging motions.

Rare Collectibles

1. Penny Black Stamp: The world's first adhesive postage stamp, issued in 1840 in the United Kingdom.

2. Honus Wagner Baseball Card: One of the rarest and most valuable baseball cards, issued in the early 1900s.

3. Double Eagle Coin: A $20 gold coin minted in 1933, extremely rare due to most being melted down.

4. Action Comics #1: The first appearance of Superman, a highly prized comic book.

5. Inverted Jenny Stamp: A postage stamp error featuring an upside-down airplane, highly sought after by collectors.

6. Blue Mauritius Stamp: One of the rarest stamps in the world, issued in 1847.

7. Mona Lisa: While not for sale, it's considered one of the most valuable and recognized art pieces in the world.

8. Stradivarius Violins: Renowned for their exceptional sound quality and craftsmanship, made in the 17th and 18th centuries.

9. First Edition Books: Rare first editions, such as "Harry Potter and the Philosopher's Stone," can fetch high prices.

10. Fabergé Eggs: Elaborate jeweled eggs created by the House of Fabergé for Russian tsars.

11. Vintage Wines: Rare bottles of wine, such as a 1945 Château Mouton-Rothschild, can be extremely valuable.

12. Antique Furniture: Pieces from renowned makers like Thomas Chippendale or Duncan Phyfe are highly collectible.

13. Sports Memorabilia: Items like Babe Ruth's bat or Muhammad Ali's gloves are prized by collectors.

14. Ancient Coins: Coins from ancient civilizations, such as a Roman denarius, are sought after by numismatists.

15. Vintage Automobiles: Classic cars like a 1962 Ferrari 250 GTO are incredibly valuable.

16. Original Movie Posters: Posters from classic films like "Casablanca" or "Metropolis" are highly collectible.

17. Historical Documents: Items like the Magna Carta or a signed copy of the Declaration of Independence are priceless.

18. Rare Gems: Unique gemstones like the Hope Diamond are famous and highly valuable.

19. Vintage Toys: Early editions of toys like the original Barbie doll or Star Wars action figures can fetch high prices.

20. Autographs: Signatures of historical figures, such as Abraham Lincoln or William Shakespeare, are highly prized.

Artistic Techniques

1. Fresco: A technique of mural painting executed upon freshly laid lime plaster, commonly used during the Renaissance.

2. Impressionism: A 19th-century art movement characterized by small, thin brush strokes and an emphasis on the accurate depiction of light.

3. Cubism: An early 20th-century avant-garde art movement that brought European painting and sculpture historically forward.

4. Pointillism: A technique of painting in which small, distinct dots of color are applied in patterns to form an image.

5. Sfumato: An Italian term meaning "smoky," referring to the technique of blending colors and tones, famously used by Leonardo da Vinci.

6. Chiaroscuro: The use of strong contrasts between light and dark to give the illusion of volume in modeling three-dimensional objects and figures.

7. Trompe-l'œil: A technique that uses realistic imagery to create the optical illusion that depicted objects exist in three dimensions.

8. Mosaic: Art consisting of patterns or images made of small pieces of colored stone, glass, or other materials.

9. Graffiti Art: Street art created using spray paint or other materials, often with bold colors and designs.

10. Lithography: A printing process that uses a flat stone or metal plate to apply images to paper or other materials.

11. Etching: A printmaking technique where an image is incised into a surface, typically using acid to create a design on a metal plate.

12. Woodcut: A relief printing technique where an image is carved into the surface of a block of wood.

13. Stippling: The creation of a pattern simulating varying degrees of solidity or shading by using small dots.

14. Digital Art: Art created using digital technology, including software and computer graphics.

15. Collage: An artistic composition made by adhering various materials such as paper, cloth, or found objects to a surface.

16. Assemblage: An artistic form or medium usually created on a defined substrate that consists of three-dimensional elements projecting out of or from the substrate.

17. Decoupage: The art of decorating an object by gluing colored paper cutouts onto it in combination with special paint effects.

18. Impasto: A technique where paint is laid on an area of the surface very thickly, so that the brush or palette knife strokes are visible.

19. Encaustic Painting: Also known as hot wax painting, it involves using heated beeswax to which colored pigments are added.

20. Stencil: A technique for reproducing designs by passing ink or paint over holes cut in cardboard or metal onto the surface to be decorated.

Global Festivals

1. Carnival in Rio de Janeiro: The world's largest carnival, famous for its parades, samba music, and vibrant costumes.

2. Diwali: The Hindu festival of lights celebrated across India and by Indian communities worldwide.

3. Chinese New Year: Also known as the Spring Festival, celebrated with fireworks, dragon dances, and family reunions.

4. Oktoberfest: A beer festival held annually in Munich, Germany, attracting millions of visitors.

5. Holi: The Indian festival of colors, celebrating the arrival of spring with colored powders and water.

6. Mardi Gras in New Orleans: Famous for its parades, beads, and vibrant street parties.

7. La Tomatina: Held in Buñol, Spain, where participants throw tomatoes at each other in a massive food fight.

8. Running of the Bulls: Part of the San Fermín festival in Pamplona, Spain, where participants run in front of a group of bulls.

9. Day of the Dead (Día de los Muertos): A Mexican holiday honoring deceased loved ones with altars, food, and marigolds.

10. Glastonbury Festival: One of the largest music and performing arts festivals in the world, held in the UK.

11. Hanami: The Japanese tradition of viewing cherry blossoms in spring, often accompanied by picnics.

12. St. Patrick's Day: Celebrated worldwide to honor the patron saint of Ireland, featuring parades and green attire.

13. Eid al-Fitr: The Muslim festival marking the end of Ramadan, celebrated with feasts and giving to charity.

14. Burning Man: An annual event in Nevada's Black Rock Desert, known for its art installations and communal living.

15. Venice Carnival: Known for its elaborate masks and costumes, held annually in Venice, Italy.

16. Harbin Ice Festival: Held in Harbin, China, featuring massive ice sculptures and winter activities.

17. Up Helly Aa: A Viking fire festival held in Shetland, Scotland, involving torchlight processions and burning a Viking ship.

18. Lunar New Year: Celebrated in various Asian countries, marking the start of the lunar calendar year.

19. Inti Raymi: An ancient Incan festival in Peru, celebrating the sun god Inti.

20. Bastille Day: France's national day on July 14th, commemorated with fireworks and parades.

Military Innovations

1. Chariot: First used in Mesopotamia around 3000 BCE, the chariot revolutionized ancient warfare with its speed and mobility.

2. Phalanx Formation: Developed by the ancient Greeks, this military formation of heavily armed foot soldiers provided great defensive strength.

3. Stirrup: Introduced by the Chinese in the 4th century AD, it allowed riders to use weapons more effectively while mounted.

4. Gunpowder: Invented in China in the 9th century, it led to the development of firearms and explosives.

5. Longbow: Used effectively by the English in the 14th and 15th centuries, particularly in battles like Agincourt.

6. Bayonet: A blade attached to the muzzle of a rifle, turning it into a spear for close combat.

7. Ironclad Warships: Introduced during the American Civil War, these ships had iron or steel armor plating.

8. Trench Warfare: Prominently used during World War I, involving soldiers fighting from extensive networks of trenches.

9. Blitzkrieg: A German tactic in World War II involving rapid, coordinated attacks using aircraft, tanks, and infantry.

10. Nuclear Weapons: Developed during World War II, with the first use on Hiroshima and Nagasaki in 1945.

11. Drones: Unmanned aerial vehicles used for reconnaissance and targeted strikes, increasingly common in modern warfare.

12. Stealth Technology: Aircraft like the F-117 Nighthawk use technology to avoid detection by radar.

13. Night Vision: Devices developed to allow soldiers to see in low-light conditions.

14. GPS: Originally developed by the U.S. military, it allows precise location tracking and navigation.

15. Missile Defense Systems: Technologies like the Patriot missile system designed to detect and destroy incoming missiles.

16. Biometric Identification: Used for secure access and identification, involving fingerprints, retinal scans, and facial recognition.

17. Cyber Warfare: The use of digital attacks against enemy information systems.

18. Railgun: An electromagnetic projectile launcher capable of firing at extremely high velocities.

19. Exoskeletons: Wearable suits designed to enhance a soldier's strength and endurance.

20. Laser Weapons: Directed energy weapons that use focused light to damage or destroy targets.

Technology Advancements

1. Internet: Developed from ARPANET in the 1960s, it revolutionized communication and information sharing.

2. Smartphones: Devices that combine a phone, computer, camera, and various sensors into one portable unit.

3. Artificial Intelligence: AI systems like neural networks and machine learning algorithms that perform tasks typically requiring human intelligence.

4. 3D Printing: A process that creates three-dimensional objects layer by layer from a digital model.

5. Blockchain: A decentralized ledger technology that underpins cryptocurrencies like Bitcoin.

6. CRISPR: A gene-editing technology that allows scientists to alter DNA sequences with high precision.

7. Renewable Energy: Technologies like solar panels and wind turbines that generate energy from renewable sources.

8. Electric Vehicles: Cars powered by electricity instead of traditional internal combustion engines.

9. Wearable Technology: Devices like smartwatches and fitness trackers that monitor health and activity.

10. Quantum Computing: Advanced computing using the principles of quantum mechanics to process information.

11. Virtual Reality (VR): Immersive simulations created using computer technology, used in gaming, training, and therapy.
12. Augmented Reality (AR): Technology that overlays digital information onto the real world, used in applications like gaming and navigation.

13. Nanotechnology: The manipulation of matter on an atomic or molecular scale, used in medicine, electronics, and materials science.

14. Autonomous Vehicles: Self-driving cars and drones that operate without human intervention.

15. Smart Home Technology: Devices like smart thermostats and security systems that can be controlled remotely.

16. Telemedicine: The use of telecommunication technology to provide medical care remotely.

17. 5G Networks: The fifth generation of mobile network technology, offering faster speeds and more reliable connections.

18. Biometric Security: Security systems that use physical characteristics like fingerprints or facial recognition for identification.

19. Voice Assistants: AI-powered devices like Amazon's Alexa and Google Assistant that respond to voice commands.

20. Space Exploration: Advancements like reusable rockets developed by companies like SpaceX, reducing the cost of space travel.

Cinematic Trivia

1. The First Film: The first moving picture was "Roundhay Garden Scene" by Louis Le Prince in 1888.

2. Longest Film: "Logistics" is the longest film ever made, with a runtime of 857 hours (35 days and 17 hours).

3. Most Expensive Film: "Pirates of the Caribbean: On Stranger Tides" had a production budget of $379 million.

4. Highest Grossing Film: As of 2021, "Avengers: Endgame" is the highest-grossing film of all time, earning over $2.798 billion worldwide.

5. First Sound Film: "The Jazz Singer" (1927) is considered the first feature-length motion picture with synchronized dialogue.

6. First Color Film: The first feature-length color film was "The World, the Flesh and the Devil" (1914).

7. Longest Running Film Franchise: The James Bond series, starting with "Dr. No" in 1962, is one of the longest-running film franchises.

8. Most Oscars Won by a Film: "Ben-Hur" (1959), "Titanic" (1997), and "The Lord of the Rings: The Return of the King" (2003) each won 11 Oscars.

9. Animated Films: "Toy Story" (1995) was the first entirely computer-animated feature film.

10. Silent Films: "The Artist" (2011) is one of the few modern silent films and won the Academy Award for Best Picture.

11. Method Acting: Daniel Day-Lewis is known for his method acting, including living in a wheelchair for "My Left Foot."

12. Cameo Appearances: Alfred Hitchcock made cameo appearances in 39 of his films.

13. Improv in Film: The famous line "Here's looking at you, kid" from "Casablanca" was improvised by Humphrey Bogart.

14. Longest Continuous Shot: "Russian Ark" (2002) is a film made from a single 96-minute continuous shot.

15. Film Locations: "The Lord of the Rings" trilogy was filmed entirely in New Zealand.

16. Iconic Props: The sled "Rosebud" from "Citizen Kane" is one of the most famous props in film history.

17. Oscar Hosts: Bob Hope hosted the Academy Awards 19 times, more than anyone else.

18. Special Effects: "Star Wars" revolutionized special effects with its use of motion control photography.

19. Box Office Bombs: "Cleopatra" (1963) nearly bankrupted 20th Century Fox despite being one of the highest-grossing films of the year.

20. Film Festivals: The Cannes Film Festival, established in 1946, is one of the most prestigious film festivals in the world.

Philosophical Ideas

1. Plato's Allegory of the Cave: Suggests that the reality perceived by our senses is just a shadow of the true reality.

2. Aristotle's Golden Mean: Advocates for finding a moderate position between extremes.

3. Descartes' Cogito, Ergo Sum: "I think, therefore I am," positing that thinking is proof of existence.

4. Kant's Categorical Imperative: States that one should act only according to that maxim whereby you can at the same time will that it should become a universal law.

5. Utilitarianism: Proposed by Jeremy Bentham and John Stuart Mill, advocating for the greatest good for the greatest number.

6. Existentialism: Emphasized by Jean-Paul Sartre, focusing on individual freedom, choice, and existence.

7. Nihilism: The belief that life is without objective meaning, purpose, or intrinsic value.

8. Hegel's Dialectic: A three-step process of thesis, antithesis, and synthesis to understand the development of ideas.

9. Confucianism: Emphasizes moral integrity, family loyalty, and respect for elders.

10. Stoicism: Advocates for self-control, rationality, and virtue as the path to happiness.

11. Epicureanism: Founded by Epicurus, teaching that pleasure is the greatest good but should be pursued in moderation.

12. Taoism: Philosophical system advocating living in harmony with the Tao, the fundamental nature of the universe.

13. Buddhism: Focuses on the Four Noble Truths and the Eightfold Path as a way to end suffering.

14. Hedonism: The pursuit of pleasure and intrinsic goods as the primary or most important goals of human life.

15. Marxism: Developed by Karl Marx, focuses on the role of class struggle in societal development and advocates for a classless society.

16. Deconstruction: A philosophical approach developed by Jacques Derrida that questions the ability of language to represent reality.

17. Rationalism: Emphasizes reason as the primary source of knowledge, as opposed to empiricism.

18. Transcendentalism: A philosophical movement that developed in the 19th century, emphasizing the inherent goodness of people and nature.

19. Social Contract Theory: Developed by thinkers like Hobbes, Locke, and Rousseau, proposing that individuals consent to surrender some of their freedoms in exchange for security.

20. Pragmatism: An American philosophy that assesses the truth of beliefs by their practical consequences and applications.

Famous Trials

1. Trial of Socrates (399 BC): Socrates was tried and sentenced to death for impiety and corrupting the youth of Athens.

2. Trial of Joan of Arc (1431): Joan of Arc was tried for heresy and witchcraft and was burned at the stake.

3. Salem Witch Trials (1692): A series of hearings and prosecutions of people accused of witchcraft in colonial Massachusetts.

4. Trial of Galileo (1633): Galileo was tried by the Inquisition for supporting heliocentrism and was placed under house arrest.

5. Dreyfus Affair (1894): Alfred Dreyfus, a French Jewish officer, was wrongly convicted of treason, leading to a major political scandal.

6. Scopes Monkey Trial (1925): John Scopes was tried for teaching evolution in a Tennessee public school, challenging creationism laws.

7. Nuremberg Trials (1945-1946): Military tribunals held after World War II to prosecute prominent leaders of Nazi Germany.

8. Trial of Charles I (1649): The King of England was tried and executed for treason during the English Civil War.

9. Rosenberg Trial (1951): Julius and Ethel Rosenberg were tried and executed for allegedly spying for the Soviet Union.

10. O.J. Simpson Trial (1995): The trial of O.J. Simpson for the murder of his ex-wife Nicole Brown Simpson and her friend Ronald Goldman.

11. Trial of Saddam Hussein (2005-2006): Saddam Hussein was tried and executed for crimes against humanity.

12. Watergate Scandal (1973-1974): Trials and hearings leading to the resignation of President Richard Nixon.

13. Leopold and Loeb (1924): The trial of two wealthy students for the murder of a 14-year-old boy in a "perfect crime" scenario.

14. The Chicago Seven (1969-1970): Trial of seven defendants charged with conspiracy and inciting to riot during the 1968 Democratic National Convention.

15. Nelson Mandela Rivonia Trial (1963-1964): Nelson Mandela and others were tried for sabotage and conspiracy against the apartheid government.

16. Amanda Knox Trial (2007-2015): Amanda Knox was tried and eventually acquitted for the murder of her roommate Meredith Kercher in Italy.

17. Ted Bundy Trials (1976-1979): Serial killer Ted Bundy was tried and convicted for several murders.

18. The Trial of the Chicago White Sox (1921): Eight members of the Chicago White Sox were tried for allegedly fixing the 1919 World Series.

19. Lindbergh Kidnapping Trial (1935): Bruno Hauptmann was tried and convicted for the kidnapping and murder of Charles Lindbergh's baby.

20. Manson Family Trial (1970-1971): Charles Manson and his followers were tried and convicted for the murders of seven people, including actress Sharon Tate.

Great Escapes

1. The Great Escape (1944): Allied prisoners of war escaped from Stalag Luft III during World War II.

2. Alcatraz Escape (1962): Frank Morris and the Anglin brothers escaped from the infamous Alcatraz prison and were never found.

3. Escape from Sobibor (1943): A mass escape from the Sobibor extermination camp in Nazi-occupied Poland.

4. Patriots' Escape (1776): Ethan Allen and 30 American prisoners escaped from British captivity during the American Revolutionary War.

5. Libby Prison Escape (1864): More than 100 Union soldiers escaped from Libby Prison during the American Civil War.

6. Maze Prison Escape (1983): 38 IRA prisoners escaped from the Maze Prison in Northern Ireland.

7. Texas Seven (2000): Seven inmates escaped from the John B. Connally Unit in Texas, leading to a nationwide manhunt.

8. Henri Charrière ("Papillon"): Escaped from the French penal colony of Devil's Island in 1941.

9. The Swiss Soldier's Escape: Swiss officer and prisoner of war, Franz von Werra, escaped from British captivity during World War II.

10. Dietrich Bonhoeffer's Escape Plan: Although he didn't escape, he attempted to flee from Nazi persecution during World War II.

11. Escape from Dannemora (2015): Richard Matt and David Sweat escaped from Clinton Correctional Facility in New York.

12. Great Train Robbery Escape (1965): Charlie Wilson escaped from Winson Green Prison after being convicted of his role in the Great Train Robbery.

13. The Pas-de-Calais Escapes (1942-1944): A series of mass escapes from the German POW camp in Pas-de-Calais, France.

14. John Dillinger's Escape (1934): The notorious bank robber escaped from Crown Point Jail using a fake gun.

15. Harry Houdini's Escapes: Famous magician Harry Houdini was known for his incredible escapes from handcuffs, straitjackets, and sealed containers.

16. Billy the Kid (1881): Escaped from the Lincoln County jail in New Mexico, killing two deputies in the process.

17. Escape from Pretoria (1979): Tim Jenkin and Stephen Lee, anti-apartheid activists, escaped from Pretoria Central Prison in South Africa.

18. Casablanca Conference (1943): Churchill and Roosevelt planned to escape Casablanca during World War II if threatened by Axis forces.

19. HMS Scepter Escape (1781): Captain William E. Young and his crew escaped from the French-controlled island of Martinique.

20. Rudolf Vrba and Alfred Wetzler (1944): Escaped from Auschwitz and provided detailed reports of the atrocities happening there.

Astronomical Events

1. Solar Eclipse: When the moon passes between the Earth and the sun, blocking the sun's light.

2. Lunar Eclipse: When the Earth passes between the sun and the moon, casting a shadow on the moon.

3. Halley's Comet: Visible from Earth every 76 years, last seen in 1986 and next expected in 2061.

4. Supernova: A powerful and luminous explosion of a star, such as SN 1987A.

5. Aurora Borealis: Also known as the Northern Lights, caused by solar wind interacting with Earth's magnetosphere.

6. Transit of Venus: When Venus passes directly between the Earth and the sun, last occurred in 2012 and next in 2117.

7. Meteor Shower: Events like the Perseids, where numerous meteors are seen radiating from a point in the sky.

8. Blue Moon: The second full moon in a calendar month, occurring roughly every 2.7 years.

9. Blood Moon: A total lunar eclipse where the moon appears red due to sunlight scattering through Earth's atmosphere.

10. Planetary Alignment: When planets align in a straight line, such as the Great Conjunction of Jupiter and Saturn in 2020.

11. Galactic Collision: Predicted collision between the Milky Way and Andromeda galaxies in about 4 billion years.

12. Solar Flare: A sudden eruption of intense high-energy radiation from the sun's surface.

13. Black Hole Merger: The merging of two black holes, detected by gravitational waves.

14. Penumbral Lunar Eclipse: When only the outer shadow of Earth falls on the moon, causing a subtle shadow.

15. Total Solar Eclipse: The sun is completely covered by the moon, casting a shadow on Earth, like the one in 2017.

16. Comet Hale-Bopp: One of the brightest comets of the 20th century, visible in 1997.

17. Venus Retrograde: The apparent backward motion of Venus as observed from Earth.

18. Gamma-Ray Burst: Extremely energetic explosion observed in distant galaxies, believed to be associated with supernovae.

19. Quadrantid Meteor Shower: A major meteor shower that peaks in early January.

20. Jupiter's Great Red Spot: A persistent high-pressure region producing an anticyclonic storm on Jupiter.

Fascinating Flora

1. Titan Arum: Known as the corpse flower, it emits a foul odor to attract pollinators.

2. Venus Flytrap: A carnivorous plant that catches and digests insects.

3. Baobab Tree: Native to Africa, known for its massive trunk and longevity, some living over a thousand years.

4. Rafflesia Arnoldii: Produces the world's largest flower, also known for its strong odor resembling rotting flesh.

5. Welwitschia Mirabilis: A desert plant native to Namibia, with only two leaves that grow continuously throughout its life.

6. Giant Sequoia: Among the largest trees in the world by volume, native to California.

7. Sensitive Plant (Mimosa Pudica): Its leaves fold inward when touched.

8. Coconut Palm: Produces coconuts, which can travel long distances by sea to germinate on distant shores.

9. Redwood Trees: The tallest trees in the world, reaching heights of over 350 feet.

10. Dragon's Blood Tree: Known for its red sap, which has been used for medicinal purposes and dyes.

11. Sundew Plant: Another carnivorous plant that traps insects with its sticky leaves.

12. Strangler Fig: Grows around a host tree, eventually enveloping and killing it.

13. Bamboo: One of the fastest-growing plants, some species can grow up to 35 inches per day.

14. Wolffia Globosa: The smallest flowering plant, also known as watermeal.

15. Corpse Flower: Produces a strong odor of rotting flesh to attract pollinators.

16. Living Stones (Lithops): Succulent plants that resemble stones or pebbles, native to southern Africa.

17. Ginkgo Biloba: One of the oldest living tree species, dating back 270 million years.

18. Ghost Orchid: A rare and endangered orchid known for its ethereal appearance and lack of leaves.

19. Rainbow Eucalyptus: Its bark peels away to reveal bright green, blue, purple, and orange layers.

20. Pitcher Plant: A carnivorous plant with modified leaves that form a deep cavity filled with digestive liquid to trap insects.

Haunted Locations

1. The Tower of London, England: Known for its long history of executions and imprisonment, it is said to be haunted by the ghosts of Anne Boleyn and other historical figures.

2. Eastern State Penitentiary, USA: This former prison in Philadelphia is rumored to be haunted by former inmates, including Al Capone.

3. Aokigahara Forest, Japan: Also known as the Suicide Forest, it is believed to be haunted by the spirits of those who have taken their own lives there.

4. The Stanley Hotel, USA: Located in Colorado, it inspired Stephen King's "The Shining" and is known for its paranormal activity.

5. Château de Brissac, France: This historic castle is said to be haunted by the "Green Lady," a ghost of a murdered noblewoman.

6. Poveglia Island, Italy: Used as a quarantine station and later a mental asylum, it is considered one of the most haunted places in the world.

7. Edinburgh Castle, Scotland: A historic fortress with reports of ghostly drummers and a headless drummer.

8. The Myrtles Plantation, USA: Located in Louisiana, it is rumored to be haunted by former slaves and a young girl named Chloe.

9. Bhangarh Fort, India: An abandoned fort known for its eerie atmosphere and legends of curses.

10. Monte Cristo Homestead, Australia: Known as Australia's most haunted house, with reports of numerous spirits.

11. Highgate Cemetery, England: A famous cemetery in London with sightings of ghosts and supernatural beings.

12. Banff Springs Hotel, Canada: A historic hotel in Alberta, reputed to be haunted by numerous ghosts, including a bride who died on her wedding day.

13. Houska Castle, Czech Republic: Built over a supposed "gateway to Hell," it is said to be haunted by demonic creatures.

14. The Queen Mary, USA: A retired ocean liner now docked in Long Beach, California, known for ghostly apparitions and strange noises.

15. Hill of Crosses, Lithuania: A pilgrimage site with thousands of crosses, believed to be haunted by the spirits of those who placed them.

16. Dracula's Castle (Bran Castle), Romania: Associated with Vlad the Impaler, it is rumored to be haunted by his spirit.

17. Port Arthur, Australia: A former penal colony with reports of ghostly sightings and eerie sounds.

18. Ancient Ram Inn, England: One of the oldest buildings in Wotton-under-Edge, known for its paranormal activity.

19. Winchester Mystery House, USA: Built by Sarah Winchester, this mansion in California is famous for its labyrinthine design and ghostly encounters.

20. Leap Castle, Ireland: Known as the most haunted castle in Ireland, with reports of a violent past and numerous spirits.

Ancient Manuscripts

1. Dead Sea Scrolls: Discovered in the 1940s and 1950s, these ancient Jewish texts date back to the 3rd century BCE.

2. Codex Sinaiticus: One of the oldest complete manuscripts of the New Testament, written in the 4th century.

3. Magna Carta: A charter of rights agreed to by King John of England in 1215, influencing many constitutional documents.

4. Epic of Gilgamesh: One of the earliest works of literary fiction, written on clay tablets in ancient Mesopotamia.

5. Rosetta Stone: A granodiorite stele inscribed with a decree in three scripts, key to deciphering Egyptian hieroglyphs.

6. Book of the Dead: An ancient Egyptian funerary text containing spells to aid the dead in the afterlife.

7. Gutenberg Bible: The first major book printed using movable type, published by Johannes Gutenberg in the 15th century.

8. Domesday Book: A manuscript record of the "Great Survey" of much of England and parts of Wales completed in 1086.

9. Voynich Manuscript: An illustrated codex written in an unknown script and language, its purpose and origin are still debated.

10. Emerald Tablet: An ancient text attributed to Hermes Trismegistus, foundational to Western alchemy.

11. Codex Gigas: Also known as the "Devil's Bible," this 13th-century manuscript is famous for its large size and a full-page illustration of the Devil.

12. Nag Hammadi Library: A collection of early Christian and Gnostic texts discovered in Egypt in 1945.

13. Qur'an: The holy book of Islam, believed to have been revealed to the Prophet Muhammad in the 7th century.

14. Tibetan Book of the Dead: A Tibetan Buddhist text that describes the experiences of the consciousness after death.

15. Illuminated Manuscripts: Medieval manuscripts decorated with gold or silver, such as the Book of Kells.

16. Epic of Manas: A traditional epic poem of the Kyrgyz people, passed down orally for centuries before being transcribed.

17. Sanskrit Vedas: The oldest scriptures of Hinduism, composed in early Sanskrit over 3,000 years ago.

18. Beowulf Manuscript: An Old English epic poem written in the early medieval period, one of the most important works of Anglo-Saxon literature.

19. Celtic Ogham Stones: Standing stones inscribed with the early medieval alphabet used primarily to write the early Irish language.

20. Homer's Iliad and Odyssey: Ancient Greek epic poems attributed to Homer, fundamental to Western literature.

Global Cuisines

1. Italian Cuisine: Known for dishes like pasta, pizza, and risotto, often featuring ingredients like tomatoes, olive oil, and cheese.

2. French Cuisine: Famous for its culinary techniques, pastries, and dishes like escargot, coq au vin, and croissants.

3. Japanese Cuisine: Includes sushi, sashimi, tempura, and ramen, often emphasizing fresh, seasonal ingredients.

4. Mexican Cuisine: Known for its bold flavors and spices, with dishes like tacos, enchiladas, and guacamole.

5. Indian Cuisine: Features a variety of spices and herbs, with popular dishes like curry, biryani, and samosas.

6. Chinese Cuisine: Diverse regional styles include Sichuan, Cantonese, and Hunan, with dishes like dumplings, Peking duck, and stir-fry.

7. Thai Cuisine: Known for its balance of sweet, sour, salty, and spicy flavors, with dishes like pad Thai, green curry, and tom yum soup.

8. Greek Cuisine: Features dishes like moussaka, souvlaki, and baklava, often using olive oil, herbs, and feta cheese.

9. Spanish Cuisine: Includes tapas, paella, and churros, with regional variations like Catalan and Basque.

10. Lebanese Cuisine: Known for mezze, tabbouleh, kibbeh, and baklava, often emphasizing fresh vegetables and herbs.

11. Brazilian Cuisine: Famous for churrasco (barbecue), feijoada (bean stew), and pão de queijo (cheese bread).

12. Moroccan Cuisine: Features tagines, couscous, and harira soup, with a rich use of spices like saffron and cinnamon.

13. Ethiopian Cuisine: Known for injera (flatbread) and wat (stew), often eaten with the hands.

14. Turkish Cuisine: Includes kebabs, meze, and baklava, with influences from Ottoman culinary traditions.

15. Vietnamese Cuisine: Features dishes like pho (noodle soup), banh mi (sandwich), and spring rolls, emphasizing fresh herbs and vegetables.

16. Peruvian Cuisine: Known for ceviche, lomo saltado, and quinoa dishes, with influences from indigenous and Spanish cooking.

17. Caribbean Cuisine: Features jerk chicken, rice and peas, and plantains, with a mix of African, European, and indigenous influences.

18. Russian Cuisine: Includes dishes like borscht (beet soup), blini (pancakes), and pelmeni (dumplings).

19. Korean Cuisine: Known for kimchi, bibimbap, and Korean barbecue, with a focus on fermented foods.

20. South African Cuisine: Features braai (barbecue), bobotie (meat pie), and biltong (dried meat), with influences from Dutch, Indian, and indigenous traditions.

Urban Legends

1. The Hookman: A classic urban legend about a couple in a car who hear a radio report about an escaped convict with a hook for a hand.

2. The Choking Doberman: A story about a couple whose dog starts choking, only to discover it was choking on the fingers of a burglar.

3. Bloody Mary: A legend that claims saying "Bloody Mary" three times in front of a mirror will summon a ghostly apparition.

4. The Vanishing Hitchhiker: A tale of a hitchhiker who disappears from the car without a trace, often leaving behind a piece of clothing.

5. The Killer in the Backseat: A story about a driver who is warned by a gas station attendant or a passing driver that there is someone hiding in the backseat.

6. The Babysitter and the Man Upstairs: A legend about a babysitter who receives threatening calls, only to find out they are coming from inside the house.

7. The Mexican Pet: A tale of a tourist who brings home a stray dog from Mexico, only to find out it's actually a giant rat.

8. Slender Man: A fictional supernatural character created as an internet meme, often depicted as a tall, faceless figure.

9. The Clown Statue: A story about a babysitter who is disturbed by a clown statue in the house, only to find out it's a person.

10. The Kidney Heist: An urban legend about a traveler who wakes up in a bathtub filled with ice, only to discover one of their kidneys has been removed.

11. The Licked Hand: A tale about a girl who thinks her dog is licking her hand at night, only to find out it's an intruder.

12. Polybius: A legend about an arcade game that supposedly caused players to suffer from seizures, nightmares, and hallucinations.

13. The Goatman: A half-man, half-goat creature said to inhabit various rural areas, often associated with bridges or tunnels.

14. The Black-Eyed Children: Stories of children with completely black eyes who appear at people's doorsteps, asking to be let in.

15. The Russian Sleep Experiment: A fictional story about Soviet researchers who kept test subjects awake for 15 days with disastrous results.

16. The Spider Bite: A legend about a person who gets bitten by a spider, only to have baby spiders hatch from the wound later.

17. The Phantom Clown Scare: Reports of creepy clowns trying to abduct children, which have surfaced in various places over the years.

18. The Haunted Road: Stories of ghostly apparitions and supernatural occurrences on certain roads, like Clinton Road in New Jersey.

19. The Wendigo: A legend from Native American folklore about a cannibalistic spirit or creature that possesses people and drives them to eat human flesh.

20. The Curse of the Crying Boy Painting: An urban legend claiming that a series of paintings of crying boys brought bad luck and fires to their owners.

Historical Mysteries

1. The Lost Colony of Roanoke: The entire population of the Roanoke Island colony vanished without a trace in the late 16th century, leaving only the word "Croatoan" carved into a post.

2. The Disappearance of Amelia Earhart: In 1937, famed aviator Amelia Earhart vanished over the Pacific Ocean during an attempt to circumnavigate the globe.

3. The Fate of the Princes in the Tower: Edward V and his brother Richard disappeared from the Tower of London in 1483, and their fate remains unknown.

4. The Mary Celeste: This American merchant ship was found adrift and abandoned in the Atlantic Ocean in 1872, with no sign of the crew.

5. The Amber Room: A room made entirely of amber panels, gold leaf, and mirrors, lost during World War II, its whereabouts are still unknown.

6. The Identity of Jack the Ripper: The true identity of the notorious serial killer who terrorized London in 1888 remains a mystery.

7. The Ark of the Covenant: According to the Bible, this sacred chest vanished from the Temple of Solomon in Jerusalem, and its fate is unknown.

8. The Library of Alexandria: Once the greatest library in the ancient world, its destruction and the loss of its vast collection of scrolls remain a mystery.

9. The Voynich Manuscript: An illustrated codex written in an unknown script and language, its purpose and meaning are still debated.

10. The Lost City of Atlantis: Described by Plato, the existence and location of this supposed advanced civilization remain speculative.

11. The Mystery of Stonehenge: The purpose and construction methods of this prehistoric monument in England are still debated.

12. The Zodiac Killer: An unidentified serial killer who operated in Northern California in the late 1960s and early 1970s, whose identity remains unknown.

13. The Bermuda Triangle: A region in the western part of the North Atlantic Ocean where ships and aircraft have mysteriously disappeared.

14. The Shroud of Turin: A linen cloth bearing the image of a man, believed by some to be Jesus Christ, but its authenticity is disputed.

15. The Wow! Signal: A strong narrowband radio signal received in 1977, its source remains unexplained.

16. The Tomb of Cleopatra: The final resting place of Cleopatra and Mark Antony has never been found.

17. The Collapse of the Maya Civilization: The reasons behind the sudden decline and abandonment of Maya cities in the 9th century are still debated.

18. The Identity of D.B. Cooper: A man who hijacked a plane in 1971, parachuted out with ransom money, and disappeared without a trace.

19. The Sphinx's Missing Nose: The Great Sphinx of Giza is missing its nose, but how and when it was lost is unknown.

20. The Tunguska Event: A massive explosion that flattened 2,000 square kilometers of forest in Siberia in 1908, believed to be caused by a meteor or comet.

Social Movements

1. The Civil Rights Movement: A struggle for social justice in the 1950s and 1960s in the United States, aiming to end racial discrimination and segregation.

2. The Women's Suffrage Movement: A decades-long fight for women's right to vote, culminating in the 19th Amendment in the U.S. in 1920.

3. The Environmental Movement: Began in the 1960s, focusing on conservation, pollution control, and public awareness of environmental issues.

4. The Anti-Apartheid Movement: A global campaign to end racial segregation and discrimination in South Africa, leading to the end of apartheid in 1994.

5. The LGBTQ+ Rights Movement: Advocates for the rights and acceptance of LGBTQ+ individuals, significantly progressing with the legalization of same-sex marriage.

6. The Labor Movement: Fought for better wages, reasonable hours, and safer working conditions, leading to significant labor laws.

7. The Anti-Vietnam War Movement: A major social movement in the 1960s and 1970s opposing U.S. involvement in the Vietnam War.

8. The Black Lives Matter Movement: Began in 2013 to combat violence and systemic racism towards Black people.

9. The #MeToo Movement: A movement against sexual harassment and assault, gaining widespread attention in 2017.

10. The Indian Independence Movement: A series of activities and campaigns aimed at ending British rule in India, led by figures like Mahatma Gandhi.

11. The Disability Rights Movement: Advocates for equal opportunities and rights for individuals with disabilities, leading to laws like the ADA in the U.S.

12. The Fair Trade Movement: Promotes better trading conditions and sustainability for producers in developing countries.

13. The Occupy Movement: A protest movement that began in 2011, focusing on economic inequality and the influence of corporations on government.

14. The Animal Rights Movement: Advocates for the ethical treatment of animals and opposes practices like factory farming and animal testing.

15. The Temperance Movement: A social movement against the consumption of alcoholic beverages, leading to Prohibition in the U.S.

16. The Abolitionist Movement: Worked to end slavery and the slave trade, leading to the abolition of slavery in various countries.

17. The Anti-Nuclear Movement: Opposes nuclear weapons and nuclear power, gaining momentum after incidents like Chernobyl and Fukushima.

18. The Youth Climate Movement: Led by young activists like Greta Thunberg, advocating for action on climate change.

19. The Indigenous Rights Movement: Advocates for the rights and recognition of indigenous peoples around the world.

20. The Human Rights Movement: Focuses on protecting and promoting human rights globally, with organizations like Amnesty International playing key roles.

Natural Disasters

1. The 2004 Indian Ocean Tsunami: Caused by a massive undersea earthquake, it killed over 230,000 people across 14 countries.

2. The 1906 San Francisco Earthquake: Devastated the city, causing fires and leaving over 80% of San Francisco in ruins.

3. Hurricane Katrina (2005): One of the deadliest hurricanes in U.S. history, causing severe flooding in New Orleans and over 1,800 deaths.

4. The 1815 Eruption of Mount Tambora: The largest volcanic eruption in recorded history, causing a "year without a summer" in 1816.

5. The Great East Japan Earthquake (2011): Triggered a powerful tsunami and the Fukushima nuclear disaster.

6. The 1755 Lisbon Earthquake: Destroyed much of Lisbon, Portugal, and caused tsunamis and fires, leading to significant loss of life.

7. The Dust Bowl (1930s): Severe dust storms in the U.S. Great Plains caused by drought and poor agricultural practices, leading to widespread displacement.

8. The 1986 Chernobyl Disaster: A catastrophic nuclear accident in Ukraine, causing long-term environmental and health effects.

9. The 1931 China Floods: Considered the deadliest natural disaster in recorded history, with estimated deaths ranging from 1 to 4 million.

10. The 1980 Eruption of Mount St. Helens: A major volcanic eruption in Washington state, causing significant damage and 57 deaths.

11. The 1883 Eruption of Krakatoa: Resulted in massive tsunamis and global climatic effects, killing over 36,000 people.

12. The 2010 Haiti Earthquake: A devastating earthquake that struck near Port-au-Prince, killing over 200,000 people.

13. The 1908 Messina Earthquake: Struck Sicily and Calabria in Italy, killing over 100,000 people.

14. The 1970 Bhola Cyclone: One of the deadliest tropical cyclones in history, hitting East Pakistan (now Bangladesh) and killing up to 500,000 people.

15. The 1923 Great Kanto Earthquake: Devastated Tokyo and Yokohama in Japan, causing over 140,000 deaths.

16. The 2008 Sichuan Earthquake: A major earthquake in China that caused nearly 90,000 deaths.

17. The 1985 Mexico City Earthquake: A devastating earthquake that caused significant damage and loss of life in Mexico's capital.

18. The 1991 Mount Pinatubo Eruption: A major volcanic eruption in the Philippines that caused global climatic effects.

19. The 2015 Nepal Earthquake: A powerful earthquake that struck near Kathmandu, causing widespread damage and over 9,000 deaths.

20. The 1942 Huaraz Avalanche: Triggered by an earthquake, this avalanche buried the Peruvian town of Huaraz, killing around 4,000 people.

Literary Classics

1. Moby-Dick by Herman Melville: A novel about the obsessive quest of Captain Ahab to hunt the white whale Moby-Dick.

2. Pride and Prejudice by Jane Austen: A romantic novel that critiques the British class system through the story of Elizabeth Bennet and Mr. Darcy.

3. To Kill a Mockingbird by Harper Lee: A novel addressing racial injustice in the American South, seen through the eyes of Scout Finch.

4. 1984 by George Orwell: A dystopian novel about a totalitarian regime that employs surveillance and propaganda to control its citizens.

5. The Great Gatsby by F. Scott Fitzgerald: A critique of the American Dream, set in the Roaring Twenties, focusing on the mysterious Jay Gatsby.

6. War and Peace by Leo Tolstoy: A historical novel that depicts the impact of the Napoleonic Wars on Russian society.

7. Jane Eyre by Charlotte Brontë: A novel about the life and struggles of an orphaned girl who becomes a governess and finds love.

8. The Catcher in the Rye by J.D. Salinger: A novel about teenage rebellion and angst, narrated by the disenchanted Holden Caulfield.

9. The Odyssey by Homer: An epic poem recounting the adventures of Odysseus as he tries to return home after the Trojan War.

10. Crime and Punishment by Fyodor Dostoevsky: A psychological novel about the moral dilemmas of a young man who commits murder.

11. The Divine Comedy by Dante Alighieri: An epic poem describing the journey through Hell, Purgatory, and Paradise.

12. Brave New World by Aldous Huxley: A dystopian novel exploring the consequences of state control, technology, and societal conditioning.

13. Anna Karenina by Leo Tolstoy: A novel about the tragic love affair of Anna Karenina, set against the backdrop of Russian society.

14. The Brothers Karamazov by Fyodor Dostoevsky: A philosophical novel exploring themes of faith, doubt, and morality.

15. Wuthering Heights by Emily Brontë: A novel about the intense and doomed love between Heathcliff and Catherine Earnshaw.

16. The Iliad by Homer: An epic poem about the Trojan War and the conflict between Achilles and Agamemnon.

17. Don Quixote by Miguel de Cervantes: A novel about the adventures of a nobleman who believes he is a knight, accompanied by his squire, Sancho Panza.

18. The Grapes of Wrath by John Steinbeck: A novel about the struggles of a poor family during the Great Depression as they migrate to California.

19. Madame Bovary by Gustave Flaubert: A novel about a doctor's wife who seeks escape from her provincial life through extramarital affairs.

20. The Picture of Dorian Gray by Oscar Wilde: A novel about a young man who remains youthful while his portrait ages and reflects his moral decay.

Art Forgery

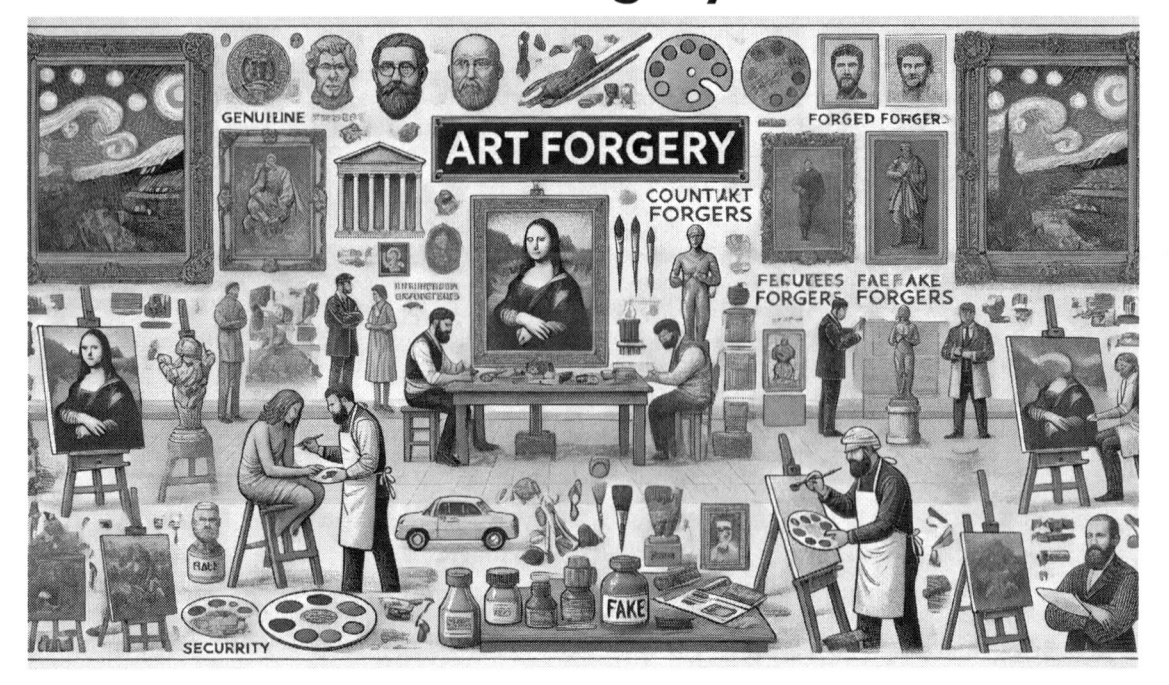

1. Han van Meegeren: One of the most famous art forgers, he created works attributed to Vermeer and sold them for millions.

2. Elmyr de Hory: A prolific art forger whose works imitating Modigliani, Picasso, and others fooled experts for years.

3. The Beltracchi Scandal: Wolfgang Beltracchi created fake paintings by many famous artists, fooling the art world for decades.

4. The Greenhalgh Family: British family of forgers who produced fake artworks, manuscripts, and sculptures.

5. The Forgery of the Turin Shroud: The Shroud of Turin, believed by some to be Jesus' burial cloth, has been suggested by some researchers to be a medieval forgery.

6. Ken Perenyi: An American artist who became a master forger, creating works that were sold as originals by many famous artists.

7. John Myatt: Created over 200 fake paintings, some of which were sold by major auction houses as genuine works.

8. Van Gogh's Fakes: Numerous fake Van Gogh paintings have surfaced, causing experts to frequently reassess his catalog.

9. Operation Bullfinch: An FBI sting operation that caught art forgers and those selling counterfeit artworks.

10. The 'Medici' Conspiracy: Art dealer Gianfranco Becchina was involved in smuggling and selling forged ancient art.

11. Tom Keating: An English artist who claimed to have forged over 2,000 paintings by more than 100 different artists.

12. Michelangelo's Forgeries: Michelangelo is said to have created a fake antique statue, which he passed off as an original.

13. The Greenhalgh's Amarna Princess: A forged statue sold to the Bolton Museum for £440,000, later revealed to be a fake.

14. Forgery in Antiquities: The art world has seen numerous fake antiquities, including coins, statues, and pottery.

15. Fake Warhols: The market for Andy Warhol's works has been flooded with fakes, prompting tighter authentication measures.

16. The Isabella Stewart Gardner Museum Heist: Although not forgery, stolen pieces are often forged to cover up the original thefts.

17. Forged Signatures: Forgers often add fake signatures to works to increase their value, such as adding Monet's name to a painting.

18. Digital Forgeries: The rise of digital art has also seen an increase in digital forgeries.

19. The FBI's Art Crime Team: Dedicated to investigating art theft and forgery in the United States.

20. Provenance Issues: Lack of proper provenance or history of ownership can make it easier for forgeries to be accepted as genuine.

Historical Art Movements

1. Renaissance: Originating in Italy in the 14th century, this movement focused on the revival of classical learning and wisdom.

2. Baroque: A highly ornate and often extravagant style of architecture, art, and music that flourished in Europe from the early 17th until the mid-18th century.

3. Rococo: An 18th-century artistic movement and style, characterized by ornate decoration, light colors, and asymmetrical designs.

4. Neoclassicism: A revival of classical art and architecture that emerged in the mid-18th century as a reaction against the Rococo style.

5. Romanticism: An artistic, literary, and intellectual movement that originated in the late 18th century, emphasizing emotion and individualism.

6. Realism: An art movement that began in the mid-19th century, focusing on depicting everyday life and society without idealization.

7. Impressionism: Developed in the late 19th century in France, characterized by small, thin brush strokes and an emphasis on light and its changing qualities.

8. Post-Impressionism: A French art movement that developed roughly between 1886 and 1905, reacting against Impressionists' concern for naturalistic depiction of light and color.

9. Symbolism: An art and literature movement that began in the late 19th century, emphasizing the use of symbols and themes of mysticism.

10. Art Nouveau: An international style of art, architecture, and applied art, especially the decorative arts, that was most popular between 1890 and 1910.

11. Fauvism: An early 20th-century movement led by Matisse, characterized by bold, often distorted forms and vivid colors.

12. Cubism: An early 20th-century avant-garde movement pioneered by Picasso and Braque, characterized by fragmented subject matter.

13. Expressionism: A modernist movement that originated in Germany in the early 20th century, presenting the world from a subjective perspective.

14. Dada: An art movement of the European avant-garde in the early 20th century, characterized by its rejection of logic and embrace of chaos and irrationality.

15. Surrealism: A 20th-century movement that sought to release the creative potential of the unconscious mind, for example by the irrational juxtaposition of images.

16. Abstract Expressionism: A post-World War II art movement in American painting, developed in New York in the 1940s.

17. Pop Art: An art movement that emerged in the 1950s and flourished in the 1960s in America and Britain, drawing inspiration from popular culture.

18. Minimalism: A movement that began in the 1960s and is characterized by simplicity and the use of monochromatic palettes.

19. Conceptual Art: Art in which the idea or concept presented by the artist is considered more important than the finished product.

20. Futurism: An early 20th-century Italian art movement that emphasized speed, technology, youth, and violence, and objects such as the car, the airplane, and the industrial city.

Modern Art

1. Jackson Pollock's Drip Paintings: Created by dripping or pouring paint onto a canvas, these works are iconic examples of Abstract Expressionism.

2. Andy Warhol's Pop Art: Known for his depictions of everyday objects like Campbell's soup cans and portraits of celebrities like Marilyn Monroe.

3. Banksy's Street Art: This anonymous artist's politically charged and often provocative works appear on walls around the world.

4. Damien Hirst's Shark: Known for his controversial works, including a tiger shark preserved in formaldehyde.

5. Yayoi Kusama's Infinity Rooms: Immersive installations that create a sense of infinite space using mirrors and light.

6. Jeff Koons' Balloon Dogs: Large, shiny sculptures that resemble balloon animals, playing with concepts of art and kitsch.

7. David Hockney's iPad Art: The British artist embraced technology, creating vibrant digital paintings using an iPad.

8. Anish Kapoor's Cloud Gate: A public sculpture in Chicago, also known as "The Bean," made of polished stainless steel.

9. Marina Abramović's Performance Art: Known for her endurance-based performances, including "The Artist Is Present" at MoMA.

10. Gerhard Richter's Abstracts: Combining photorealism and abstract art, Richter's squeegee paintings are celebrated for their color and texture.

11. Ai Weiwei's Activism: Blending art and activism, Ai's works critique social and political issues in China and globally.

12. Kara Walker's Silhouettes: Using black paper cutouts, Walker addresses themes of race, gender, and history in her installations.

13. Olafur Eliasson's Installations: Known for creating immersive environments, such as "The Weather Project" at Tate Modern.

14. Takashi Murakami's Superflat: A postmodern art movement merging traditional Japanese art with contemporary pop culture.

15. Jean-Michel Basquiat's Graffiti: Starting as a graffiti artist, Basquiat's work combines text and imagery to address social issues.

16. Jenny Holzer's Truisms: Using LED displays and projections, Holzer's works convey provocative statements and questions.

17. Tracey Emin's "My Bed": An installation featuring the artist's unmade bed, surrounded by personal items, exploring themes of intimacy and vulnerability.

18. Richard Serra's Steel Sculptures: Known for his large-scale, site-specific sculptures made from industrial materials like steel.

19. Chuck Close's Portraits: Renowned for his massive, photorealistic portraits created from grids of tiny, abstract shapes.

20. Barbara Kruger's Text-Based Art: Using bold text over black-and-white images, Kruger's works address consumerism and power dynamics.

Photographic Oddities

1. The Cottingley Fairies: Photos taken by two girls in 1917, claimed to show real fairies but later revealed as a hoax using paper cutouts.

2. The Brown Lady of Raynham Hall: A famous ghost photograph taken in 1936, allegedly showing a spectral figure descending a staircase.

3. The Loch Ness Monster: The 1934 "surgeon's photograph" purportedly showing Nessie, later revealed to be a hoax.

4. Time Traveler in 1941: A photo from the South Fork Bridge reopening in Canada shows a man dressed in modern attire, sparking time travel theories.

5. The Phantom Thumb: A photo taken during the American Civil War appears to show an extra thumb on a soldier's shoulder, a mystery of photographic error.

6. Solway Firth Spaceman: A photo taken in 1964 of a young girl appears to show a figure in a spacesuit in the background, later debunked as her mother.

7. The Tulip Staircase Ghost: A 1966 photo taken in the Queen's House in Greenwich appears to show a shrouded figure ascending the staircase.

8. The Babushka Lady: A woman seen filming during the JFK assassination who was never identified, adding to conspiracy theories.

9. The Hessdalen Lights: Mysterious lights seen in Norway, captured on film and still unexplained.

10. Freddy Jackson Ghost: A 1919 photo of a WWI squadron appears to show the ghostly image of a mechanic who had died days earlier.

11. The Mysterious Crouching Man: A photo of the 1963 assassination of South Vietnamese President Diem shows an inexplicable crouching figure.

12. The Black Knight Satellite: Photos taken by NASA allegedly show a mysterious object orbiting Earth, fueling theories of alien satellites.

13. Anomalies on Mars: Various photos taken by Mars rovers show odd shapes and figures, sparking theories of life or artifacts on Mars.

14. The Hook Island Sea Monster: A 1964 photo claimed to show a giant tadpole-like sea creature, later thought to be a hoax or misidentified object.

15. The SS Watertown Ghosts: A 1924 photo shows the faces of two dead sailors in the water, believed to be ghosts by the crew.

16. The Battle of Los Angeles: A 1942 photo shows searchlights converging on an unidentified object, believed by some to be a UFO.

17. The Fresno Nightcrawler: A video and subsequent still images show strange, legged creatures walking through a yard in Fresno, California.

18. The Skunk Ape: A 2000 photo allegedly shows a Bigfoot-like creature in the Florida Everglades.

19. Pyramid on the Moon: A photo taken during an Apollo mission appears to show a pyramid-like structure on the Moon's surface.

20. The Human Face on Mars: A 1976 Viking 1 orbiter photo shows a landform resembling a human face, later attributed to shadows and natural formations.

Musical Instruments

1. Stradivarius Violins: Made by Antonio Stradivari in the 17th and 18th centuries, these violins are renowned for their exceptional sound quality.

2. Piano: Invented by Bartolomeo Cristofori in Italy around 1700, the piano evolved from earlier keyboard instruments like the harpsichord.

3. Theremin: One of the first electronic musical instruments, controlled without physical contact, invented by Leon Theremin in 1920.

4. Sitar: A plucked string instrument used in Indian classical music, popularized globally by Ravi Shankar.

5. Didgeridoo: A wind instrument developed by Indigenous Australians, traditionally made from hardwood trees hollowed out by termites.

6. Bagpipes: A traditional instrument of Scotland, featuring a bag that holds air and multiple pipes for melody and drones.

7. Cello: Part of the violin family, the cello is known for its deep, rich tones and is a key instrument in orchestras.

8. Steelpan: Originating from Trinidad and Tobago, this percussion instrument is made from industrial drums.

9. Accordion: A portable, free-reed instrument with a keyboard and bellows, commonly used in folk and popular music.

10. Banjo: A stringed instrument associated with American folk and bluegrass music, originally derived from African instruments.

11. Ocarina: An ancient wind instrument with a history spanning thousands of years, made from materials like clay or plastic.

12. Marimba: A percussion instrument with wooden bars struck by mallets, originating from Africa and developed further in Central America.

13. Erhu: A two-stringed bowed musical instrument, sometimes known as the Chinese violin or fiddle.

14. Hurdy-Gurdy: A string instrument played by turning a wheel which rubs against the strings, popular in medieval and folk music.

15. Sousaphone: A type of tuba designed for marching bands, invented by John Philip Sousa.

16. Glass Harmonica: An instrument invented by Benjamin Franklin, consisting of glass bowls or goblets of different sizes.

17. Balalaika: A Russian stringed instrument with a distinctive triangular body, used in folk music.

18. Kalimba: Also known as the thumb piano, it is a traditional African instrument with metal tines plucked by the thumbs.

19. Uilleann Pipes: The national bagpipe of Ireland, played with a bellows strapped around the waist and arm.

20. Hang Drum: A modern instrument invented in Switzerland, resembling a steel drum and played with the hands.

Famous Museums

1. The Louvre (Paris, France): The world's largest art museum, home to the Mona Lisa and the Venus de Milo.

2. The British Museum (London, UK): Known for its vast collection of world art and artifacts, including the Rosetta Stone and the Elgin Marbles.

3. The Metropolitan Museum of Art (New York, USA): One of the largest and most comprehensive art museums in the world.

4. The Vatican Museums (Vatican City): Houses the extensive collection of art and historical artifacts amassed by the Roman Catholic Church.

5. The Uffizi Gallery (Florence, Italy): Renowned for its collection of Italian Renaissance masterpieces, including works by Botticelli and Michelangelo.

6. The Prado Museum (Madrid, Spain): Holds one of the finest collections of European art, including works by Velázquez, Goya, and El Greco.

7. The Hermitage Museum (St. Petersburg, Russia): One of the largest and oldest museums in the world, founded by Catherine the Great.

8. The Rijksmuseum (Amsterdam, Netherlands): Home to a vast collection of Dutch Golden Age paintings, including works by Rembrandt and Vermeer.

9. The Smithsonian Institution (Washington, D.C., USA): A group of museums and research institutions, including the National Air and Space Museum and the National Museum of Natural History.

10. The Guggenheim Museum (New York, USA): Known for its modern and contemporary art collection and its distinctive Frank Lloyd Wright-designed building.

11. The Acropolis Museum (Athens, Greece): Houses artifacts from the Acropolis of Athens, including the Parthenon marbles.

12. The Getty Center (Los Angeles, USA): Features European paintings, drawings, sculpture, and decorative arts.

13. The National Gallery (London, UK): Houses a rich collection of over 2,300 paintings dating from the mid-13th century to 1900.

14. The Museum of Modern Art (MoMA) (New York, USA): One of the most influential modern art museums in the world.

15. The Art Institute of Chicago (Chicago, USA): Known for its collection of Impressionist and Post-Impressionist paintings.

16. The Pergamon Museum (Berlin, Germany): Home to monumental buildings such as the Pergamon Altar and the Ishtar Gate.

17. The Victoria and Albert Museum (London, UK): The world's largest museum of decorative arts and design.

18. The National Palace Museum (Taipei, Taiwan): Houses one of the largest collections of Chinese art and artifacts.

19. The Tate Modern (London, UK): A major gallery of international modern and contemporary art.

20. The Musée d'Orsay (Paris, France): Located in a former railway station, it is renowned for its collection of Impressionist and Post-Impressionist masterpieces.

Unique Hobbies

1. Extreme Ironing: Combining the thrills of extreme outdoor activities with the mundane task of ironing clothes.

2. Geocaching: A global treasure hunt where participants use GPS coordinates to find hidden containers called geocaches.

3. Soap Carving: The art of carving intricate designs and sculptures out of bars of soap.

4. Toy Voyaging: Sending a toy on a journey around the world, documenting its travels through photos and stories.

5. Mushroom Foraging: The practice of hunting for wild mushrooms in forests and fields.

6. Urban Exploration: Exploring abandoned buildings and structures, often photographing the experience.

7. Sandcastle Building: Creating elaborate and detailed sand sculptures on the beach.

8. Ferret Legging: A bizarre sport where participants place live ferrets inside their trousers and see who can endure the longest.

9. Tree Shaping: The practice of training living trees into artistic shapes and structures.

10. Hikaru Dorodango: A Japanese art form of creating shiny, polished balls from mud and dirt.

11. Ant Keeping: Raising and caring for ant colonies as a hobby, often involving elaborate ant farms.

12. Competitive Duck Herding: Using trained dogs to herd ducks through obstacle courses.

13. Soap Bubble Art: Creating large and colorful soap bubbles, often used in performances and competitions.

14. Gongoozling: Watching activity on canals, particularly the movement of boats and wildlife.

15. LARPing (Live Action Role-Playing): Participants physically act out characters and scenarios, often in elaborate costumes.

16. Beekeeping: Maintaining bee colonies to produce honey and beeswax, and for the benefits of pollination.

17. Candle Making: Crafting candles in various shapes, sizes, and scents as a creative and relaxing activity.

18. Juggling: The skill of keeping several objects, such as balls or clubs, in the air by continuously tossing and catching them.

19. Trainspotting: Observing and recording details about trains and railways, often as part of a larger interest in rail transport.

20. Soap Making: Creating custom soaps with unique colors, fragrances, and ingredients.

Animal Behavior

1. Migration: Many animals, such as birds, whales, and butterflies, migrate long distances seasonally for breeding or food.

2. Hibernation: Animals like bears and bats enter a state of deep sleep during winter to conserve energy.

3. Mimicry: Some animals, like the mimic octopus, can imitate the appearance and behavior of other species for protection.

4. Tool Use: Certain animals, such as chimpanzees and crows, use tools to help them gather food or solve problems.

5. Altruism: Behaviors seen in animals like dolphins and ants, where individuals help others at a cost to themselves.

6. Communication: Animals use various methods to communicate, such as the complex vocalizations of whales and the dances of bees.

7. Camouflage: Many animals, like chameleons and octopuses, can change their appearance to blend into their environment.

8. Social Hierarchies: Species like wolves and chickens establish pecking orders to maintain social structure.

9. Courtship Rituals: Birds of paradise and peacocks perform elaborate displays to attract mates.

10. Symbiosis: Mutualistic relationships, such as clownfish living in sea anemones, benefit both parties involved.

11. Imprinting: Young animals, such as ducklings, form attachments and follow the first moving object they see, usually their mother.

12. Parental Care: Many animals, like penguins and elephants, invest significant time and effort in raising their young.

13. Territoriality: Animals like lions and wolves defend specific areas against intruders to protect their resources.

14. Play Behavior: Seen in many mammals, such as dolphins and primates, playing helps develop social and physical skills.

15. Nocturnal Activity: Animals like owls and bats are active at night and have adaptations to thrive in the dark.

16. Migration: Monarch butterflies travel thousands of miles from North America to central Mexico each year.

17. Echolocation: Bats and dolphins emit sounds and listen for the echoes to navigate and hunt.

18. Pack Hunting: Predators like wolves and orcas hunt in groups to take down larger prey.

19. Molting: Animals like snakes and crustaceans shed their outer layer to grow.

20. Nest Building: Birds, insects, and other animals construct nests to protect their eggs and young.

Marine Life

1. Great Barrier Reef: The largest coral reef system in the world, located off the coast of Queensland, Australia, and visible from space.

2. Blue Whale: The largest animal on Earth, reaching lengths of up to 100 feet and weighing as much as 200 tons.

3. Jellyfish: Some jellyfish are immortal, capable of reverting to their juvenile form after reaching maturity.

4. Octopus: Known for their intelligence, octopuses can solve puzzles, use tools, and escape from enclosures.

5. Deep-Sea Vents: Hydrothermal vents on the ocean floor support unique ecosystems with organisms that rely on chemosynthesis.

6. Bioluminescence: Many marine organisms, such as certain jellyfish and plankton, can produce their own light through chemical reactions.

7. Sharks: Sharks have been around for over 400 million years, predating dinosaurs by millions of years.

8. Coral Bleaching: When stressed by changes in conditions such as temperature, light, or nutrients, corals expel the symbiotic algae living in their tissues, causing them to turn white.

9. Sea Turtles: Sea turtles can live up to 100 years and migrate thousands of miles between feeding grounds and nesting sites.

10. Marine Biodiversity: Oceans cover more than 70% of the Earth's surface and contain 94% of the Earth's living species.

11. Mangroves: These coastal trees can survive in saltwater and protect shorelines from erosion and storm surges.

12. Marine Mammals: Species like dolphins, whales, and seals are adapted to living in the marine environment, with specialized lungs and insulating blubber.

13. Seahorses: Male seahorses are the ones that become pregnant and give birth to young.

14. Polar Bears: Though not truly marine animals, polar bears depend on sea ice to hunt seals.

15. Giant Squid: One of the largest invertebrates, capable of reaching lengths of up to 43 feet.

16. Plastic Pollution: Millions of tons of plastic end up in the oceans each year, posing a significant threat to marine life.

17. Overfishing: Many fish populations are declining due to overfishing, which disrupts marine ecosystems.

18. Dolphin Communication: Dolphins use complex vocalizations and body language to communicate with each other.

19. Symbiosis: Clownfish and sea anemones have a mutualistic relationship where the fish get protection from predators, and the anemones get cleaned.

20. Seagrass Meadows: Important underwater habitats that support diverse marine life and help maintain water quality.

Aviation Facts

1. First Flight: The Wright brothers made their first powered flight on December 17, 1903, in Kitty Hawk, North Carolina.

2. Supersonic Flight: The Concorde was a supersonic passenger airliner that could travel faster than the speed of sound.

3. Largest Passenger Plane: The Airbus A380 is the world's largest passenger airliner, capable of carrying up to 853 passengers.

4. Black Box: Airplanes are equipped with flight data recorders and cockpit voice recorders, commonly known as black boxes, to investigate accidents.

5. Stealth Technology: Stealth aircraft, like the B-2 Spirit, are designed to avoid detection by radar.

6. Longest Flight: Singapore Airlines Flight SQ23 is the longest non-stop flight in the world, covering approximately 9,534 miles from New York to Singapore.

7. Jet Engines: Frank Whittle in the UK and Hans von Ohain in Germany independently developed the jet engine during World War II.

8. Vertical Takeoff: The Harrier Jump Jet is capable of vertical takeoff and landing, allowing it to operate in confined spaces.

9. Space Shuttle: The Space Shuttle was a reusable spacecraft used by NASA for missions between 1981 and 2011.

10. Boeing 747: Known as the "Queen of the Skies," it was the first wide-body airplane and held the passenger capacity record for 37 years.

11. Amelia Earhart: In 1932, she became the first woman to fly solo nonstop across the Atlantic Ocean.

12. SR-71 Blackbird: The fastest jet aircraft, capable of speeds over Mach 3, used for reconnaissance missions.

13. First Commercial Flight: The first scheduled commercial flight took place on January 1, 1914, between St. Petersburg and Tampa, Florida.

14. Autopilot: Modern airplanes use advanced autopilot systems to assist with navigation and control during flight.

15. Air Traffic Control: The first air traffic control tower was established at Cleveland Municipal Airport in 1930.

16. Skydiving: Skydivers jump from aircraft at high altitudes, free-fall, and deploy parachutes to land safely.

17. Hot Air Balloons: The Montgolfier brothers made the first manned hot air balloon flight in 1783.

18. Drones: Unmanned aerial vehicles (UAVs) are used for various purposes, including surveillance, delivery, and photography.

19. Zero Gravity: Parabolic flights, often called "vomit comets," simulate zero gravity for astronauts and researchers.

20. Solar-Powered Flight: Solar Impulse 2 completed the first solar-powered flight around the world in 2016.

Astronomy

1. The Milky Way: Our galaxy, the Milky Way, contains over 200 billion stars and is approximately 100,000 light-years in diameter.

2. Black Holes: Regions of space where gravity is so strong that nothing, not even light, can escape.

3. The Sun: A medium-sized star located at the center of our solar system, composed mainly of hydrogen and helium.

4. Exoplanets: Planets outside our solar system, with thousands discovered orbiting other stars.

5. Light Year: The distance light travels in one year, approximately 5.88 trillion miles.

6. The Big Bang: The theory that the universe began as a singularity and has been expanding ever since, approximately 13.8 billion years ago.

7. Supernova: A massive explosion that occurs when a star exhausts its nuclear fuel and collapses.

8. The Hubble Space Telescope: Launched in 1990, it has provided some of the most detailed images of distant galaxies and nebulae.

9. Galaxies: There are estimated to be over 2 trillion galaxies in the observable universe.

10. Pulsars: Highly magnetized, rotating neutron stars that emit beams of electromagnetic radiation.

11. Andromeda Galaxy: The closest spiral galaxy to the Milky Way, on a collision course with our galaxy in about 4 billion years.

12. Dark Matter: An unknown form of matter that makes up about 27% of the universe, detectable only through its gravitational effects.

13. Dark Energy: A mysterious force causing the accelerated expansion of the universe, making up about 68% of the universe.

14. Asteroids: Rocky objects orbiting the sun, primarily found in the asteroid belt between Mars and Jupiter.

15. Comets: Icy bodies that release gas and dust, forming a glowing coma and tail when they approach the sun.

16. Red Giants: A phase in the life cycle of a star where it expands and cools after exhausting its hydrogen fuel.

17. Neutron Stars: Extremely dense remnants of supernova explosions, composed almost entirely of neutrons.

18. The Kuiper Belt: A region beyond Neptune's orbit containing many small icy bodies, including dwarf planets like Pluto.

19. The Oort Cloud: A hypothetical distant cloud of icy objects surrounding the solar system, believed to be the source of long-period comets.

20. The Drake Equation: An equation proposed by Frank Drake to estimate the number of active, communicative extraterrestrial civilizations in the Milky Way.

Ethnobotany

1. Ayahuasca: A traditional Amazonian brew used in spiritual ceremonies, containing DMT and other psychoactive compounds.

2. Quinine: Derived from the bark of the cinchona tree, it was the first effective treatment for malaria.

3. Willow Bark: Contains salicin, a precursor to aspirin, and has been used for centuries to relieve pain and inflammation.

4. Kava: A plant from the South Pacific used to make a calming and sedative beverage.

5. Turmeric: A spice from the ginger family, used in traditional medicine for its anti-inflammatory and antioxidant properties.

6. Coca Plant: The leaves are used by Andean cultures for their stimulant effects and were historically used to make cocaine.

7. Neem: A tree whose leaves, bark, and oil are used in traditional Indian medicine for their antibacterial and antifungal properties.

8. Ginseng: A root used in traditional Chinese medicine for its purported energy-boosting and stress-relieving effects.

9. Peyote: A cactus containing mescaline, used in Native American religious ceremonies.

10. Tea Tree Oil: Extracted from the leaves of Melaleuca alternifolia, used for its antiseptic and anti-inflammatory properties.

11. Maize: A staple crop domesticated in Mexico, crucial to the diets and cultures of many indigenous peoples in the Americas.

12. Hoodia: A succulent plant used by the San people of the Kalahari Desert to suppress appetite on long hunting trips.

13. St. John's Wort: A plant used in traditional medicine for its antidepressant properties.

14. Basil: A herb sacred in Hindu culture, used in cooking and traditional medicine for its purported healing properties.

15. Yarrow: Used by various cultures for its wound-healing and anti-inflammatory properties.

16. Camu Camu: A fruit from the Amazon rainforest, known for its high vitamin C content and traditional use in medicine.

17. Ashwagandha: An herb used in Ayurvedic medicine to reduce stress and improve cognitive function.

18. Moringa: A tree whose leaves are used in traditional medicine for their nutritional and medicinal properties.

19. Sage: Used in Native American smudging ceremonies to cleanse and purify spaces.

20. Ginkgo Biloba: An ancient tree whose leaves are used in traditional Chinese medicine to improve memory and circulation.

Political Intrigue

1. Watergate Scandal: In the 1970s, President Richard Nixon's administration was involved in a break-in at the Democratic National Committee headquarters, leading to Nixon's resignation.

2. Iran-Contra Affair: In the 1980s, senior U.S. officials secretly facilitated the sale of arms to Iran, which was under an arms embargo, and used the proceeds to fund Contra rebels in Nicaragua.

3. The Dreyfus Affair: A political scandal in France in the late 19th century, where Jewish officer Alfred Dreyfus was wrongfully convicted of treason, highlighting deep-seated anti-Semitism.

4. The Assassination of Archduke Franz Ferdinand: His assassination in 1914 led to the outbreak of World War I.

5. The Teapot Dome Scandal: A bribery scandal in the 1920s involving the Harding administration and oil companies, considered one of the biggest presidential scandals before Watergate.

6. The Profumo Affair: A British political scandal in the 1960s involving Secretary of State for War John Profumo and his affair with Christine Keeler, which compromised national security.

7. The Affair of the Diamond Necklace: A scandal in the late 18th century involving Queen Marie Antoinette of France, which further tarnished her reputation and fueled revolutionary sentiments.

8. The Bay of Pigs Invasion: A failed U.S. invasion of Cuba in 1961 intended to overthrow Fidel Castro, resulting in political embarrassment for the Kennedy administration.

9. The Monica Lewinsky Scandal: In the 1990s, President Bill Clinton was impeached for perjury and obstruction of justice related to his extramarital affair with White House intern Monica Lewinsky.

10. The Enron Scandal: In 2001, the American energy company Enron was involved in corporate fraud, leading to its bankruptcy and the loss of thousands of jobs and pensions.

11. The Chappaquiddick Incident: In 1969, Senator Ted Kennedy was involved in a car accident that resulted in the death of Mary Jo Kopechne, raising questions about his conduct and character.

12. The Rosenberg Trial: In the 1950s, Julius and Ethel Rosenberg were convicted and executed for espionage for allegedly passing atomic secrets to the Soviet Union.

13. The Tammany Hall Scandal: In the late 19th century, the Tammany Hall political machine in New York City was involved in widespread corruption and graft.

14. The Spiro Agnew Resignation: Vice President Spiro Agnew resigned in 1973 amid charges of tax evasion and money laundering from his time as Governor of Maryland.

15. The Panama Papers: In 2016, a leak of documents from Panamanian law firm Mossack Fonseca revealed widespread global tax evasion and corruption involving numerous politicians and celebrities.

16. The Cambridge Analytica Scandal: In 2018, it was revealed that the political consulting firm Cambridge Analytica harvested data from millions of Facebook users without their consent to influence elections.

17. The Grigory Rasputin Influence: In early 20th century Russia, Rasputin, a mystic, gained significant influence over the Russian royal family, contributing to the political instability that led to the Russian Revolution.

18. The Jefferson-Hemings Controversy: President Thomas Jefferson was rumored to have had a long-term relationship and children with his slave Sally Hemings.

19. The Keating Five Scandal: In the late 1980s, five U.S. senators were implicated in a corruption scandal involving the Lincoln Savings and Loan Association.

20. The Snowden Revelations: In 2013, Edward Snowden leaked classified NSA documents revealing extensive global surveillance programs.

Global Conflicts

1. World War I (1914-1918): A global war originating in Europe, involving many world powers, and leading to significant political changes and the Treaty of Versailles.

2. World War II (1939-1945): A global conflict involving most of the world's nations, resulting in significant loss of life and the Holocaust.

3. The Cold War (1947-1991): A state of political and military tension between the United States and the Soviet Union, characterized by espionage, propaganda, and proxy wars.

4. The Korean War (1950-1953): A conflict between North Korea, supported by China and the Soviet Union, and South Korea, supported by the United Nations, primarily the United States.

5. The Vietnam War (1955-1975): A prolonged conflict between communist North Vietnam and South Vietnam, supported by the United States, leading to significant casualties and protests.

6. The Gulf War (1990-1991): A conflict triggered by Iraq's invasion of Kuwait, leading to a coalition force led by the United States to liberate Kuwait.

7. The Yugoslav Wars (1991-2001): A series of ethnic conflicts and wars of independence in the former Yugoslavia, resulting in the breakup of the country.

8. The Rwandan Genocide (1994): A mass slaughter of Tutsi in Rwanda by ethnic Hutus, leading to the deaths of an estimated 800,000 people.

9. The Iraq War (2003-2011): Initiated by the United States and its allies to overthrow Saddam Hussein, leading to prolonged conflict and instability in Iraq.

10. The Syrian Civil War (2011-present): An ongoing conflict between the Syrian government and various opposition groups, resulting in significant casualties and a humanitarian crisis.

11. The Falklands War (1982): A conflict between Argentina and the United Kingdom over the Falkland Islands, resulting in a British victory.

12. The Six-Day War (1967): A brief but intense conflict between Israel and neighboring Arab states, resulting in significant territorial gains for Israel.

13. The Iran-Iraq War (1980-1988): A protracted conflict between Iran and Iraq, resulting in massive casualties and economic damage.

14. The Bosnian War (1992-1995): Part of the Yugoslav Wars, involving ethnic cleansing and significant humanitarian issues.

15. The War in Afghanistan (2001-2021): Initiated by the United States in response to the 9/11 attacks, aimed at dismantling al-Qaeda and removing the Taliban from power.

16. The Russian-Georgian War (2008): A brief conflict between Russia and Georgia over the breakaway regions of South Ossetia and Abkhazia.

17. The Israeli-Palestinian Conflict: An ongoing struggle between Israelis and Palestinians over land and sovereignty in the Middle East.

18. The Mexican Drug War (2006-present): A conflict between the Mexican government and various drug trafficking cartels, resulting in significant violence and casualties.

19. The Libyan Civil War (2011): A conflict that led to the overthrow of Muammar Gaddafi and ongoing instability in Libya.

20. The Congo Wars (1996-2003): A series of conflicts involving multiple African nations and armed groups, resulting in millions of deaths and widespread displacement.

Espionage

1. Mata Hari: A famous Frisian female spy during World War I, executed by the French for espionage for Germany.

2. The Cambridge Five: A group of British double agents who passed information to the Soviet Union during and after World War II.

3. Julius and Ethel Rosenberg: Executed in 1953 for passing atomic secrets to the Soviet Union.

4. Aldrich Ames: A CIA officer who spied for the Soviet Union and Russia, compromising numerous CIA operatives.

5. Kim Philby: A high-ranking member of British intelligence who spied for the Soviet Union.

6. Operation Fortitude: A World War II deception operation by the Allies to mislead the Germans about the D-Day invasion.

7. The Enigma Code: The German cipher machine code cracked by Alan Turing and his team at Bletchley Park during World War II.

8. The Venona Project: A U.S. counterintelligence program that decrypted Soviet messages, revealing espionage activities.

9. The Glomar Explorer: A ship built by the CIA to recover a sunken Soviet submarine in the 1970s.

10. The U-2 Incident: In 1960, an American U-2 spy plane was shot down over the Soviet Union, leading to the capture of pilot Francis Gary Powers.

11. Anna Chapman: A Russian spy who was part of a sleeper cell in the United States, arrested in 2010.

12. The Berlin Tunnel: A Cold War operation where the CIA and MI6 built a tunnel to tap Soviet communications in East Berlin.

13. The Black Tom Explosion: A 1916 sabotage by German agents in the U.S., targeting munitions destined for the Allies.

14. Klaus Fuchs: A physicist who worked on the Manhattan Project and passed atomic secrets to the Soviet Union.

15. The Walker Spy Ring: A U.S. Navy officer, John Walker, who led a spy ring that sold secrets to the Soviet Union for nearly two decades.

16. The Clandestine Service: The branch of the CIA responsible for covert operations and espionage.

17. The Stasi: The East German secret police known for their extensive surveillance and espionage activities.

18. Operation Mincemeat: A British deception operation in World War II using a corpse with fake documents to mislead the Germans about the Allied invasion of Sicily.

19. The Dreyfus Affair: A political scandal in France involving a Jewish officer wrongfully convicted of espionage.

20. The Cambridge Five: A group of British spies who worked for the Soviet Union during and after World War II, including Kim Philby.

Historical Buildings

1. The Great Wall of China: A series of fortifications built over centuries to protect China from invasions, stretching over 13,000 miles.

2. The Colosseum: An ancient amphitheater in Rome, Italy, built in AD 70-80, used for gladiatorial contests and public spectacles.

3. The Eiffel Tower: A wrought-iron lattice tower in Paris, France, completed in 1889 and originally criticized before becoming a global icon.

4. The Taj Mahal: A white marble mausoleum in Agra, India, built by Mughal Emperor Shah Jahan in memory of his wife Mumtaz Mahal.

5. Machu Picchu: An ancient Incan city located in the Andes Mountains of Peru, built in the 15th century.

6. The Parthenon: A former temple on the Acropolis of Athens, Greece, dedicated to the goddess Athena and completed in 438 BC.

7. The Pyramids of Giza: Ancient pyramid structures in Egypt, built as tombs for pharaohs and considered one of the Seven Wonders of the Ancient World.

8. The Hagia Sophia: Originally a Byzantine cathedral, later an Ottoman mosque, and now a museum in Istanbul, Turkey, built in AD 537.

9. The Forbidden City: A palace complex in Beijing, China, serving as the Chinese imperial palace from the Ming dynasty to the end of the Qing dynasty.

10. Stonehenge: A prehistoric monument in Wiltshire, England, consisting of a ring of standing stones, built around 3000 BC.

11. The Leaning Tower of Pisa: A freestanding bell tower in Pisa, Italy, known for its unintended tilt, completed in the 14th century.

12. The Alhambra: A palace and fortress complex in Granada, Spain, built during the mid-14th century by the Nasrid dynasty.

13. The Kremlin: A fortified complex in Moscow, Russia, serving as the residence of the President of Russia and housing historic buildings.

14. Notre-Dame Cathedral: A medieval Catholic cathedral in Paris, France, famous for its Gothic architecture and the 2019 fire.

15. The Palace of Versailles: A royal château in Versailles, France, known for its opulent architecture and gardens, expanded by Louis XIV.

16. The Sydney Opera House: An iconic performing arts center in Sydney, Australia, designed by Jørn Utzon and opened in 1973.

17. The Louvre Museum: Originally a royal palace, now the world's largest art museum, located in Paris, France.

18. Petra: An archaeological site in Jordan, known for its rock-cut architecture and water conduit system, established around the 6th century BC.

19. The Sagrada Familia: An unfinished basilica in Barcelona, Spain, designed by architect Antoni Gaudí, construction began in 1882.

20. The Tower of London: A historic castle on the north bank of the River Thames in central London, known for its role as a royal palace, prison, and treasury.

Linguistic Evolution

1. Proto-Indo-European Language: The hypothetical ancestor of many modern languages, including English, Spanish, and Hindi, believed to have been spoken around 6,000 years ago.

2. Great Vowel Shift: A major change in the pronunciation of English vowels that took place between the 15th and 18th centuries, significantly altering the English language.

3. Pidgins and Creoles: Pidgins are simplified languages that develop between groups with no common language, which can evolve into creoles, fully developed languages spoken by native speakers.

4. Grimm's Law: Describes the systematic phonetic changes that occurred in the development of the Germanic languages from Proto-Indo-European.

5. Old English: The earliest form of the English language, spoken in England from approximately the 5th to the 12th centuries.

6. Loanwords: Many modern languages borrow words from other languages; for example, English has borrowed words like "ballet" from French and "piano" from Italian.

7. Language Isolates: Languages that have no known relatives, such as Basque in Europe or Ainu in Japan.

8. Glottalization: The use of the glottal stop in various languages, like the Cockney accent in English or the Hawaiian language.

9. The Rosetta Stone: A key artifact in deciphering Egyptian hieroglyphs, as it contained the same text in Greek, Demotic, and hieroglyphic script.

10. Cognates: Words in different languages that have a common origin, like "mother" in English and "mutter" in German.

11. Linguistic Relativity: The theory that the structure of a language affects its speakers' worldview, also known as the Sapir-Whorf hypothesis.

12. Phoneme: The smallest unit of sound that can distinguish meaning in a language, like the difference between "pat" and "bat" in English.

13. Rebus Principle: Using pictures to represent sounds, foundational to the development of written languages.

14. Sign Languages: Complete, natural languages with their own syntax and grammar, such as American Sign Language (ASL).

15. Nostratic Hypothesis: A controversial theory suggesting a common ancestral language for many language families, including Indo-European and Afro-Asiatic.

16. Language Death: When a language loses all its native speakers, such as Latin evolving into the Romance languages.

17. Neologisms: Newly coined words or expressions that may eventually become part of the standard language, like "selfie" or "googling."

18. Morphology: The study of the structure and form of words in a language, including prefixes, suffixes, and root words.

19. Dialect Continuum: A range of dialects spoken across a region, each slightly different from the next, such as the dialects of German.

20. Linguistic Reconstruction: The method of recreating the features of a language's ancestor by comparing its descendants.

Ethnomusicology

1. Gamelan: Traditional ensemble music of Indonesia, featuring instruments like metallophones, xylophones, and drums.

2. Mbira: A traditional African instrument, also known as a thumb piano, used in Shona music of Zimbabwe.

3. Tuvan Throat Singing: A style of overtone singing from Tuva, where the singer produces multiple pitches simultaneously.

4. Raga: A framework for improvisation in Indian classical music, defining the scales, motifs, and mood.

5. Didgeridoo: An ancient wind instrument developed by Indigenous Australians, traditionally made from termite-hollowed eucalyptus.

6. Polyrhythm: The use of two or more conflicting rhythms, common in African and African diaspora music.

7. Klezmer: A musical tradition of the Ashkenazi Jews of Eastern Europe, characterized by expressive melodies and modes.

8. Taiko Drumming: Traditional Japanese drumming, often featuring large drums and synchronized choreography.

9. Balafon: A wooden xylophone from West Africa, traditionally played in Mali, Burkina Faso, and Guinea.

10. Samba: A Brazilian music genre and dance style with African roots, often performed during Carnival.

11. Native American Flute: Used by various Native American tribes, known for its distinctive sound and spiritual significance.

12. Carnatic Music: One of the two main traditions of Indian classical music, originating from South India.

13. Celtic Music: Traditional music from the Celtic regions of Europe, including Ireland, Scotland, and Brittany.

14. Mariachi: A traditional form of Mexican music featuring ensembles of violins, guitars, trumpets, and singers.

15. Fado: A genre of Portuguese music characterized by melancholic tunes and lyrics, often about the sea or the life of the poor.

16. Reggae: A music genre originating from Jamaica, characterized by a rhythmic style with accents on the off-beat.

17. Balinese Kecak: A form of vocal music and dance from Bali, often referred to as the "monkey chant."

18. Griot Tradition: West African historians, storytellers, and musicians who preserve oral traditions through music and poetry.

19. Bluegrass: A genre of American roots music that developed in the 1940s, influenced by Irish, Scottish, and English music traditions.

20. Sufi Music: Devotional music of the Sufis, characterized by mystical themes and often performed at spiritual gatherings called "Sama."

Meteorology

1. The Water Cycle: The continuous movement of water on, above, and below the surface of the Earth, involving processes like evaporation, condensation, and precipitation.

2. Jet Streams: Fast-flowing, narrow air currents found in the atmospheres of some planets, including Earth, that influence weather patterns.

3. El Niño: A climate pattern that describes the unusual warming of surface waters in the eastern tropical Pacific Ocean, affecting global weather.

4. Doppler Radar: A specialized radar that measures the velocity of precipitation, helping meteorologists predict severe weather events like tornadoes.

5. Tropical Cyclones: Powerful, rotating storm systems with low pressure centers, known as hurricanes in the Atlantic and typhoons in the Pacific.

6. The Beaufort Scale: A scale for measuring wind speed, developed in 1805 by Sir Francis Beaufort.

7. Auroras: Natural light displays in the Earth's sky, predominantly seen in high-latitude regions, caused by the collision of solar wind particles with the atmosphere.

8. Atmospheric Pressure: The pressure exerted by the weight of the atmosphere, measured with a barometer.

9. The Coriolis Effect: The deflection of moving objects caused by the rotation of the Earth, influencing wind and ocean currents.

10. Cloud Types: Classified into categories such as cumulus, stratus, cirrus, and nimbus based on their appearance and altitude.

11. Greenhouse Effect: The trapping of heat in the Earth's atmosphere by greenhouse gases like carbon dioxide and methane, contributing to global warming.

12. The Ozone Layer: A layer in the Earth's stratosphere that absorbs most of the Sun's ultraviolet radiation, protecting living organisms from harmful UV rays.

13. Monsoons: Seasonal wind patterns that cause wet and dry seasons, notably affecting South Asia.

14. Foehn Winds: Warm, dry winds descending on the leeward side of mountains, known for causing rapid temperature increases.

15. The Saffir-Simpson Scale: A 1 to 5 rating based on a hurricane's sustained wind speeds, estimating potential property damage.

16. Cold Fronts: Boundaries between cold and warm air masses, often bringing abrupt weather changes like thunderstorms.

17. Heatwaves: Prolonged periods of excessively hot weather, which can have significant impacts on health, agriculture, and infrastructure.

18. Fog Formation: Occurs when water vapor condenses into tiny liquid water droplets suspended in the air near the ground.

19. The Butterfly Effect: A concept in chaos theory suggesting that small changes in initial conditions can lead to vastly different outcomes in weather patterns.

20. Weather Satellites: Orbiting devices that monitor Earth's weather and climate, providing data for forecasting and research.

Epidemiology

1. John Snow and Cholera: Known as the father of modern epidemiology, John Snow traced the source of a cholera outbreak in London to a contaminated water pump in 1854.

2. The Spanish Flu: The 1918 influenza pandemic infected about one-third of the world's population, resulting in an estimated 50 million deaths.

3. Herd Immunity: Occurs when a significant portion of a population becomes immune to a disease, reducing its spread.

4. The Black Death: A devastating pandemic that struck Europe in the 14th century, caused by the bacterium Yersinia pestis, killing an estimated 25-30 million people.

5. The Smallpox Eradication: Smallpox is the only human disease to have been eradicated, with the last natural case occurring in 1977 due to a successful global vaccination campaign.

6. The R Number: Represents the average number of people to whom a single infected person will transmit a disease, crucial for understanding epidemic dynamics.

7. Contact Tracing: A method used to identify and notify individuals who have been exposed to an infectious disease, helping to prevent further spread.

8. Zoonotic Diseases: Infections that are transmitted from animals to humans, such as rabies, Ebola, and COVID-19.

9. Epidemiological Triad: A model used to understand the interaction between the agent, host, and environment in the spread of disease.

10. The 2009 H1N1 Pandemic: Also known as the swine flu, this global outbreak was caused by a new influenza virus and resulted in widespread illness and fatalities.

11. Antimicrobial Resistance: The ability of microbes to resist the effects of drugs, making infections harder to treat and leading to higher medical costs and mortality.

12. Vector-Borne Diseases: Infections transmitted by vectors such as mosquitoes, ticks, and fleas, including malaria, Lyme disease, and Zika virus.

13. The Ebola Outbreak: The 2014-2016 West Africa Ebola outbreak was the largest in history, with over 11,000 deaths.

14. Polio Eradication: Ongoing global efforts have reduced polio cases by over 99% since 1988, with the disease now endemic in only a few countries.

15. Chronic Diseases: Conditions like heart disease, diabetes, and cancer, which are long-lasting and generally progress slowly.

16. The HIV/AIDS Pandemic: Since the 1980s, HIV/AIDS has affected millions worldwide, with significant efforts in prevention, treatment, and education.

17. Surveillance Systems: Public health systems used to monitor and respond to disease outbreaks, such as the Centers for Disease Control and Prevention (CDC) in the U.S.

18. The 2003 SARS Outbreak: Severe Acute Respiratory Syndrome, caused by a coronavirus, led to a global outbreak with significant mortality but was contained through public health measures.

19. Vaccination Programs: Immunization efforts have significantly reduced or eradicated diseases like measles, mumps, rubella, and polio.

20. The Role of WHO: The World Health Organization coordinates international public health efforts, responding to health emergencies and promoting health equity.

Urban Planning

1. Ancient Urban Planning: The city of Mohenjo-Daro in the Indus Valley Civilization had a sophisticated grid layout and advanced drainage systems dating back to 2500 BCE.

2. New York's Central Park: Designed by Frederick Law Olmsted and Calvert Vaux, Central Park was one of the first landscaped public parks in the United States.

3. Garden Cities: Ebenezer Howard proposed the Garden City movement in the late 19th century, combining the benefits of the countryside and urban life.

4. Zoning Laws: Zoning regulations control land use in urban areas, separating residential, commercial, and industrial zones to organize city development.

5. Greenbelts: These are undeveloped areas surrounding urban regions intended to limit urban sprawl and provide space for recreation and nature.

6. Smart Cities: Incorporate technology and data to improve the efficiency of urban services like traffic management, energy use, and public safety.

7. Transit-Oriented Development (TOD): Focuses on creating urban spaces that maximize access to public transportation, reducing reliance on cars.

8. Sustainable Urban Planning: Emphasizes reducing environmental impact through green building practices, renewable energy, and efficient resource use.

9. The "15-Minute City" Concept: Aims to ensure that all necessary services and amenities are within a 15-minute walk or bike ride from homes.

10. Urban Heat Islands: Cities often experience higher temperatures than rural areas due to human activities and materials that absorb and retain heat.

11. Jane Jacobs: An influential urbanist whose book "The Death and Life of Great American Cities" argued for mixed-use development and vibrant street life.

12. Le Corbusier: A pioneering architect and urban planner known for his modernist visions, including the "Radiant City" concept of high-density living.

13. Copenhagen's Bicycle Culture: Approximately 62% of Copenhagen's residents commute by bike daily, thanks to extensive cycling infrastructure.

14. The High Line: A public park built on a historic freight rail line elevated above the streets on Manhattan's West Side.

15. Masdar City: A planned city in Abu Dhabi designed to be a hub for clean technology and renewable energy, aiming to be carbon-neutral.

16. Curitiba's BRT System: Curitiba in Brazil implemented one of the first bus rapid transit (BRT) systems, significantly improving public transport efficiency.

17. Urban Agriculture: Incorporates farming into city planning, providing fresh produce, reducing food miles, and creating green spaces.

18. Gentrification: The process by which urban areas are revitalized, often leading to increased property values and displacement of lower-income residents.

19. Participatory Planning: Engages community members in the urban planning process to ensure that development meets their needs and preferences.

20. Eco-Cities: Designed with sustainable features like renewable energy, green buildings, and waste recycling, aiming to minimize ecological footprints.

Material Science

1. Graphene: A single layer of carbon atoms arranged in a hexagonal lattice, known for its incredible strength, conductivity, and flexibility.

2. Aerogel: Often called "frozen smoke," it is a lightweight material with extremely low density and excellent insulating properties.

3. Shape Memory Alloys: Metals like Nitinol can return to their original shape after being deformed when exposed to a certain temperature.

4. Superconductors: Materials that conduct electricity without resistance at extremely low temperatures, enabling powerful magnets and efficient power lines.

5. Kevlar: A high-strength synthetic fiber used in bulletproof vests and other protective gear due to its high tensile strength-to-weight ratio.

6. Carbon Nanotubes: Cylindrical nanostructures with remarkable mechanical, electrical, and thermal properties, used in a wide range of applications.

7. Metamaterials: Engineered materials with properties not found in nature, used to create invisibility cloaks and superlenses.

8. Biodegradable Plastics: Designed to decompose more quickly in the environment, reducing the impact of plastic waste.

9. Piezoelectric Materials: Generate an electric charge in response to mechanical stress, used in sensors, actuators, and energy harvesting devices.

10. Hydrogels: Water-absorbing polymers used in medical applications, agriculture, and hygiene products like contact lenses and diapers.

11. Transparent Aluminum: Also known as aluminum oxynitride, a strong, durable, and transparent material used in military and industrial applications.

12. Self-Healing Materials: Can automatically repair damage, extending the lifespan of products like coatings, concrete, and polymers.

13. Aerographite: One of the lightest materials known, made from a network of carbon nanotubes, with potential applications in lightweight structures.

14. Ferromagnetic Materials: Materials like iron, cobalt, and nickel that can be magnetized, used in electric motors and transformers.

15. Biocompatible Materials: Used in medical implants and devices, designed to interact safely with the human body.

16. Phase-Change Materials: Store and release thermal energy during phase transitions, used for temperature regulation in buildings and textiles.

17. Nanocomposites: Combine nanoparticles with bulk materials to enhance properties like strength, conductivity, and thermal resistance.

18. Photonic Crystals: Structures that control the flow of light, used in optical fibers and lasers.

19. Smart Glass: Glass that can change its light transmission properties in response to an external stimulus, used in energy-efficient windows.

20. Bulk Metallic Glasses: Amorphous metals with a disordered atomic structure, known for their strength and resistance to deformation.

Quantum Physics

1. Quantum Entanglement: A phenomenon where particles become linked, and the state of one instantly influences the state of another, regardless of distance.

2. Heisenberg Uncertainty Principle: States that it is impossible to simultaneously know both the position and momentum of a particle with absolute precision.

3. Wave-Particle Duality: Particles like electrons exhibit both wave-like and particle-like properties, depending on the experimental setup.

4. Quantum Tunneling: The ability of particles to pass through a barrier that they classically shouldn't be able to, used in devices like tunnel diodes.

5. Superposition Principle: A fundamental concept where a quantum system can exist in multiple states at once until it is measured.

6. Schrödinger's Cat: A thought experiment illustrating quantum superposition, where a cat in a box is simultaneously alive and dead until observed.

7. Quantum Computing: Uses qubits that can exist in superposition, potentially solving certain problems much faster than classical computers.

8. Quantum Cryptography: Utilizes principles of quantum mechanics to create theoretically secure communication methods.

9. Quantum Decoherence: The process by which a quantum system loses its quantum behavior and becomes classical due to interaction with its environment.

10. Bell's Theorem: Demonstrates that certain predictions of quantum mechanics are incompatible with local hidden variable theories.

11. Quantum Teleportation: The transfer of quantum information from one particle to another without physical transfer of the particles themselves.

12. Planck's Constant: A fundamental constant in quantum mechanics that relates the energy of a photon to its frequency.

13. Casimir Effect: A quantum force arising from vacuum fluctuations between two closely spaced conductive plates.

14. Quantum Field Theory: A theoretical framework combining quantum mechanics and special relativity to describe the behavior of fields and particles.

15. Dirac Equation: A relativistic equation describing the behavior of fermions, predicting the existence of antimatter.

16. Quantum Electrodynamics (QED): The quantum theory of electromagnetic interactions, explaining phenomena like the Lamb shift and electron anomalous magnetic moment.

17. Hawking Radiation: Theoretical radiation predicted to be emitted by black holes due to quantum effects near the event horizon.

18. Quantum Zeno Effect: The phenomenon where frequent observation of a quantum system can prevent it from evolving.

19. Bose-Einstein Condensate: A state of matter formed at near absolute zero, where particles occupy the same quantum state and exhibit macroscopic quantum phenomena.

20. Feynman Diagrams: Graphical representations used in particle physics to visualize and calculate interactions between particles.

Nanotechnology

1. Nanoparticles: Particles between 1 and 100 nanometers in size, used in medicine, electronics, and materials science for their unique properties.

2. Carbon Nanotubes: Cylindrical nanostructures with exceptional strength, electrical conductivity, and thermal properties, used in various applications.

3. Quantum Dots: Semiconductor nanoparticles that exhibit quantum mechanical properties, used in display technology and medical imaging.

4. Nanoscale Self-Assembly: The process by which molecules spontaneously form organized structures without human intervention, used in material science.

5. Nanomedicine: The application of nanotechnology in medicine, including targeted drug delivery and imaging.

6. Nanocomposites: Materials that combine nanoparticles with bulk materials to enhance properties like strength, conductivity, and thermal resistance.

7. Nanolithography: Techniques for creating extremely small patterns on a substrate, essential for the production of integrated circuits.

8. Graphene: A single layer of carbon atoms arranged in a hexagonal lattice, known for its exceptional electrical, mechanical, and thermal properties.

9. Nanorobots: Tiny robots designed for tasks like medical diagnostics, drug delivery, and environmental monitoring at the nanoscale.

10. Surface Plasmon Resonance: The resonant oscillation of conduction electrons at the surface of a metal nanoparticle, used in biosensing and imaging.

11. Nanotubes in Energy Storage: Used in batteries and supercapacitors to increase energy density and improve performance.

12. Dendrimers: Branched macromolecules with a tree-like structure, used in drug delivery, imaging, and as catalysts.

13. Nanofibers: Fibers with diameters in the nanometer range, used in filtration, tissue engineering, and protective clothing.

14. Molecular Electronics: The use of molecules to create electronic components, potentially leading to smaller and more efficient devices.

15. Fullerenes: Carbon molecules in the shape of a hollow sphere, tube, or ellipsoid, with applications in materials science and medicine.

16. Nanosensors: Sensors at the nanoscale capable of detecting chemical, biological, or physical changes with high sensitivity.

17. Nanoporous Materials: Materials with pore sizes in the nanometer range, used in catalysis, separation processes, and drug delivery.

18. Spintronics: A technology that exploits the intrinsic spin of electrons and its associated magnetic moment, used in advanced memory devices.

19. Photonic Crystals: Nanoscale structures that control the flow of light, used in optical communications and sensors.

20. Nanotoxicology: The study of the toxicity of nanomaterials, crucial for ensuring the safe use of nanotechnology in various applications.

Human Evolution

1. Homo Sapiens: Modern humans, Homo sapiens, evolved around 300,000 years ago in Africa.

2. Lucy: One of the most famous early human ancestors, a 3.2-million-year-old Australopithecus afarensis skeleton discovered in Ethiopia.

3. Neanderthals: Homo neanderthalensis, our closest extinct relatives, lived in Europe and Asia until about 40,000 years ago.

4. Out of Africa Theory: Suggests that modern humans originated in Africa and migrated to other parts of the world around 60,000 years ago.

5. Denisovans: An extinct species or subspecies of archaic humans, known from a few bones and DNA evidence found in Siberia.

6. Tool Use: Early humans started using stone tools about 2.6 million years ago, marking the beginning of the Paleolithic era.

7. Bipedalism: Walking on two legs is a defining characteristic of hominins, with evidence dating back over 4 million years.

8. Brain Size: The human brain has tripled in size over the course of evolution, with significant increases in Homo erectus and Homo sapiens.

9. Control of Fire: Homo erectus is believed to have been the first to control fire, around 1 million years ago, aiding in cooking and protection.

10. Art and Symbolism: The earliest known cave art, found in Spain and Indonesia, is at least 40,000 years old.

11. Language Development: The evolution of complex language is unique to humans, with the FOXP2 gene playing a crucial role.

12. Social Structures: Early human societies were likely organized in small, nomadic groups that relied on hunting and gathering.

13. Interbreeding: Modern humans interbred with Neanderthals and Denisovans, with many people today carrying small percentages of their DNA.

14. Agricultural Revolution: About 10,000 years ago, humans began transitioning from nomadic lifestyles to settled agricultural communities.

15. Clothing: Evidence of early clothing dates back to around 170,000 years ago, essential for surviving in colder climates.

16. Domestication of Animals: Dogs were likely the first domesticated animals, with evidence suggesting domestication occurred over 15,000 years ago.

17. Migration to the Americas: The first humans arrived in the Americas via a land bridge called Beringia around 15,000 years ago.

18. Homo floresiensis: A small-statured human species, nicknamed "hobbits," lived on the Indonesian island of Flores until about 50,000 years ago.

19. Homo habilis: Known as "handy man," one of the earliest members of the genus Homo, lived around 2.4 to 1.4 million years ago.

20. Oldowan Tools: The oldest-known stone tools, dating back to 2.6 million years ago, associated with Homo habilis and Australopithecus garhi.

Forensic Science

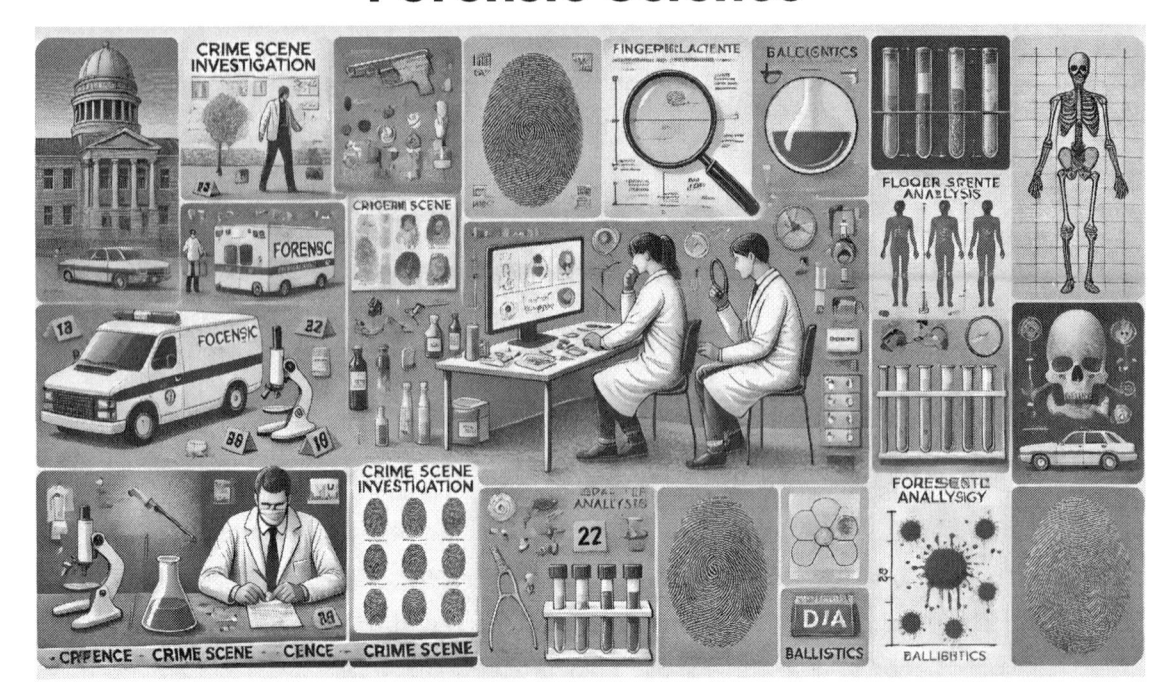

1. DNA Profiling: Revolutionized forensic science in the 1980s, allowing for the identification of individuals based on genetic material.

2. Fingerprint Analysis: No two people have identical fingerprints, making them a crucial tool for identification in criminal investigations.

3. Forensic Anthropology: The study of human skeletal remains to determine identity, cause of death, and other forensic details.

4. Ballistics: The analysis of bullets and firearms to link them to crimes, helping solve cases involving shootings.

5. Toxicology: The study of chemicals, drugs, and poisons in the body, crucial for determining causes of death and substance abuse.

6. Forensic Entomology: The use of insect evidence to estimate the time of death and other details in criminal investigations.

7. Blood Spatter Analysis: The study of bloodstains at crime scenes to reconstruct events and determine the type of weapon used.

8. Cyber Forensics: The recovery and analysis of data from electronic devices to investigate cybercrimes and digital evidence.

9. Forensic Odontology: The use of dental records and bite marks for identification and solving crimes.

10. Forensic Pathology: The examination of bodies to determine the cause of death, typically through autopsies.

11. Hair and Fiber Analysis: The examination of hair and textile fibers to link suspects to crime scenes.

12. Forensic Psychology: The application of psychology to understand criminal behavior, assess suspects, and provide expert testimony.

13. Forensic Archaeology: The use of archaeological techniques to locate and excavate human remains in criminal investigations.

14. Voice Analysis: The study of voice recordings to identify speakers and authenticate audio evidence.

15. Forensic Accounting: The investigation of financial records to detect fraud, embezzlement, and other financial crimes.

16. Facial Reconstruction: The recreation of a person's face from their skeetal remains to aid in identification.

17. Forensic Document Examination: The analysis of handwriting, ink, paper, and other document features to detect forgery and authenticate documents.

18. Forensic Botany: The study of plant evidence to link suspects to crime scenes and estimate time of death.

19. Gait Analysis: The study of a person's walking pattern to identify suspects from surveillance footage.

20. Latent Prints: Invisible fingerprints left on surfaces, made visible through chemical and physical methods for identification.

Paleontology

1. Fossil Formation: Fossils are formed when organisms are buried by sediment and minerals replace their bones over millions of years.

2. Dinosaur Extinction: Most scientists believe that a massive asteroid impact caused the extinction of the dinosaurs 66 million years ago.

3. Lucy: A 3.2-million-year-old Australopithecus afarensis skeleton discovered in Ethiopia, providing crucial insights into early human evolution.

4. Jurassic Period: Known for its large dinosaurs like Brachiosaurus and Stegosaurus, it occurred around 201 to 145 million years ago.

5. Trilobites: Extinct marine arthropods that lived for over 270 million years and are commonly found as fossils.

6. Ice Age Megafauna: Large animals like mammoths, mastodons, and saber-toothed cats roamed the Earth during the last Ice Age.

7. Amber Fossils: Fossilized tree resin that often contains well-preserved insects, plants, and other small organisms.

8. Mary Anning: A pioneering paleontologist who discovered the first complete Ichthyosaurus and several other important fossils in the early 19th century.

9. Pangaea: A supercontinent that existed around 335 to 175 million years ago before breaking apart into the continents we know today.

10. Coelacanth: A "living fossil" fish thought to have been extinct for 66 million years until one was found alive in 1938.

11. Cambrian Explosion: A period around 541 million years ago when most major animal phyla appeared in the fossil record.

12. Megalosaurus: The first dinosaur genus to be scientifically described, named by William Buckland in 1824.

13. Homo naledi: A recently discovered human ancestor with both primitive and modern traits, found in South Africa's Rising Star Cave system.

14. Fossil Record Gaps: Incomplete fossil records due to the rarity of fossilization and the need for specific conditions for fossils to form.

15. Archaeopteryx: Often considered the first bird, it had features of both dinosaurs and modern birds, dating back to the Late Jurassic period.

16. Mesozoic Era: Known as the "Age of Reptiles," it includes the Triassic, Jurassic, and Cretaceous periods, lasting from about 252 to 66 million years ago.

17. Fossilized Footprints: Trace fossils that provide information about the behavior and movement of ancient animals.

18. Permian-Triassic Extinction: The largest mass extinction event in Earth's history, occurring around 252 million years ago, wiping out about 96% of marine species.

19. Paleobotany: The study of fossilized plants, which helps scientists understand ancient ecosystems and climates.

20. Fossilized Eggs: Fossilized dinosaur eggs provide insights into the reproductive behavior and development of dinosaurs.

Archaeological Finds

1. Tutankhamun's Tomb: Discovered by Howard Carter in 1922 in Egypt's Valley of the Kings, it contained a wealth of artifacts and the intact sarcophagus of the boy king.

2. Terracotta Army: Over 8,000 life-sized clay soldiers and horses buried with China's first emperor, Qin Shi Huang, discovered in 1974.

3. Pompeii: An ancient Roman city buried by the eruption of Mount Vesuvius in 79 AD, providing well-preserved insights into Roman life.

4. Machu Picchu: An Incan citadel in Peru, rediscovered by Hiram Bingham in 1911, showcasing advanced engineering and architecture.

5. Rosetta Stone: Discovered in 1799, this artifact helped scholars decipher Egyptian hieroglyphs due to its inscriptions in three scripts.

6. Dead Sea Scrolls: Ancient Jewish texts discovered in the Qumran Caves in the 1940s, providing significant religious and historical insights.

7. Gobekli Tepe: A Neolithic site in Turkey dating back to 9600 BCE, considered the world's oldest known temple complex.

8. Stonehenge: A prehistoric monument in England, its purpose remains a mystery, with theories ranging from astronomical observatory to religious site.

9. Lascaux Caves: Discovered in 1940 in France, these caves contain some of the best-preserved prehistoric cave paintings, dating back around 17,000 years.

10. The Library of Ashurbanipal: A collection of thousands of clay tablets from the 7th century BCE in Nineveh, providing insights into Assyrian culture and knowledge.

11. Nazca Lines: Large geoglyphs in Peru, created by the Nazca culture between 500 BCE and 500 CE, depicting animals, plants, and geometric shapes.

12. Clovis Points: Distinctive stone tools associated with the Clovis culture, dating back around 13,000 years, found throughout North America.

13. The Great Zimbabwe: The ruins of an ancient city in Zimbabwe, built by the Shona people between the 11th and 15th centuries, showcasing impressive stone architecture.

14. Peking Man: Homo erectus fossils discovered in Zhoukoudian, China, dating back around 750,000 years, providing insights into early human life in Asia.

15. The Antikythera Mechanism: An ancient Greek analog computer discovered in a shipwreck, used to predict astronomical positions and eclipses.

16. The Sutton Hoo Ship Burial: An Anglo-Saxon ship burial site in England, discovered in 1939, containing a wealth of artifacts from the 7th century.

17. The Cave of Altamira: Discovered in Spain, this cave contains Upper Paleolithic paintings and drawings, dating back around 36,000 years.

18. The Royal Tombs of Ur: Excavated in the 1920s and 1930s, these tombs in present-day Iraq revealed treasures and insights into Sumerian civilization.

19. Akrotiri: A Minoan Bronze Age settlement on the Greek island of Santorini, preserved by a volcanic eruption around 1600 BCE.

20. The Mask of Agamemnon: A gold funeral mask discovered by Heinrich Schliemann in Mycenae, Greece, dating back to the 16th century BCE.

Conspiracy Theories

1. Area 51: The U.S. Air Force facility in Nevada is at the center of numerous UFO and alien conspiracy theories.

2. JFK Assassination: Theories suggest various culprits behind the assassination of President John F. Kennedy in 1963, including the CIA, the Mafia, and even Vice President Lyndon B. Johnson.

3. Moon Landing Hoax: Some believe that the 1969 Apollo moon landing was staged by NASA and the U.S. government.

4. 9/11 Attacks: Conspiracy theories claim that the U.S. government had prior knowledge of the attacks or was involved in their execution.

5. New World Order: The theory posits a secretive global elite conspiring to rule the world through an authoritarian world government.

6. Illuminati: A purported secret society believed to control world affairs and influence political and financial decisions.

7. Chemtrails: Some believe that the trails left by airplanes are chemical agents being sprayed for nefarious purposes, such as mind control or population reduction.

8. Roswell Incident: The 1947 crash of an object in Roswell, New Mexico, is believed by some to be the cover-up of an extraterrestrial spacecraft.

9. The Bermuda Triangle: The area in the North Atlantic Ocean is said to be the site of numerous mysterious disappearances of ships and aircraft.

10. HAARP: The High-Frequency Active Auroral Research Program in Alaska is suspected by some of being used for weather control or mind control.

11. Paul McCartney's Death: A theory claims that Paul McCartney of The Beatles died in 1966 and was replaced by a look-alike.

12. Fluoridation: Some believe that the addition of fluoride to drinking water is a government plot to control the population.

13. Bigfoot: Believers claim that a large, ape-like creature, also known as Sasquatch, inhabits North American forests.

14. Reptilian Elite: A theory that shape-shifting reptilian aliens are controlling human governments and societies.

15. MH370 Disappearance: Theories about the 2014 disappearance of Malaysia Airlines Flight MH370 include hijacking, a secret military shootdown, and alien abduction.

16. Denver Airport: Some think that the Denver International Airport is the headquarters of the New World Order due to its mysterious artwork and underground facilities.

17. Vaccines: Anti-vaccine conspiracies claim that vaccines cause autism or are used for mind control and population reduction.

18. The Philadelphia Experiment: Allegedly, a naval destroyer escort was rendered invisible and teleported in an experiment in 1943.

19. MKUltra: A real CIA program from the 1950s to the 1970s aimed at mind control using drugs and psychological torture, fueling numerous conspiracies.

20. The Bilderberg Group: An annual private conference of political leaders and experts from industry, finance, and academia, which some believe is a secret world government.

Historical Correspondence

1. Letters of Queen Victoria: Queen Victoria wrote numerous letters during her reign, providing insight into her personal life and politics.

2. Albert Einstein and Sigmund Freud: In their 1932 correspondence, Einstein and Freud discussed the nature of war and the possibility of peace.

3. The Balfour Declaration: A 1917 letter from British Foreign Secretary Arthur Balfour expressing support for a "national home for the Jewish people" in Palestine.

4. The Zimmerman Telegram: A secret communication from Germany to Mexico during World War I proposing a military alliance against the U.S., which helped bring the U.S. into the war.

5. Thomas Jefferson and John Adams: After years of political rivalry, these Founding Fathers resumed their friendship through extensive correspondence in their later years.

6. Marie Curie and Albert Einstein: They exchanged letters discussing scientific ideas and their experiences as prominent scientists in the early 20th century.

7. The Prison Letters of Nelson Mandela: Written during his imprisonment, these letters provide a personal view of his thoughts and experiences during apartheid.

8. Vincent van Gogh and Theo van Gogh: Letters between the artist and his brother Theo reveal Vincent's struggles, thoughts on art, and mental health.

9. The Letters of Abigail and John Adams: Their correspondence offers a detailed look into the American Revolution and the early years of the United States.

10. The Letters of Rosa Luxemburg: The letters of the Marxist theorist and revolutionary provide insight into her political views and personal life.

11. Beethoven's Immortal Beloved: A mysterious letter found after Beethoven's death addressed to an "Immortal Beloved," whose identity remains debated.

12. Charles Darwin and Asa Gray: Correspondence between Darwin and American botanist Asa Gray discussing the implications of Darwin's theory of evolution.

13. The Letters of Napoleon Bonaparte: His letters to Josephine and others reveal his personal and military thoughts.

14. The Federalist Papers: Written by Alexander Hamilton, James Madison, and John Jay, these letters advocated for the ratification of the U.S. Constitution.

15. The Gandhi-Irwin Correspondence: Letters between Mahatma Gandhi and British Viceroy Lord Irwin discussing India's independence movement.

16. Frederick Douglass' Letters: The letters of the former slave and abolitionist provide insight into his fight for civil rights and equality.

17. The Letters of Emily Dickinson: The reclusive poet's letters reveal her thoughts on life, poetry, and her personal relationships.

18. The Letters of Winston Churchill and Franklin D. Roosevelt: Their wartime correspondence reveals the close relationship between the two leaders during WWII.

19. The Letters of Anne Frank: In her diary, Anne included letters to a fictional friend, providing a poignant view of her life in hiding during the Holocaust.

20. The Love Letters of Henry VIII and Anne Boleyn: These letters reveal the passionate and tumultuous relationship that led to the creation of the Church of England.

Mythical Creatures

1. Unicorn: A legendary horse-like creature with a single horn, symbolizing purity and grace in various cultures.

2. Dragon: Mythical creatures appearing in folklore around the world, often depicted as large, serpent-like beings with the ability to breathe fire.

3. Phoenix: A mythical bird that regenerates or is reborn from its ashes, symbolizing immortality and renewal.

4. Kraken: A giant sea monster from Scandinavian folklore, said to dwell off the coast of Norway and Greenland.

5. Bigfoot: Also known as Sasquatch, a large, ape-like creature purportedly inhabiting the forests of North America.

6. Chupacabra: A creature from Latin American folklore, described as a blood-sucking animal that preys on livestock.

7. Griffin: A mythical creature with the body of a lion and the head and wings of an eagle, symbolizing strength and vigilance.

8. Basilisk: A legendary reptile in European mythology, believed to cause death with a single glance.

9. Yeti: Also known as the Abominable Snowman, a large, ape-like creature said to inhabit the Himalayan mountains.

10. Mermaid: A mythical aquatic creature with the upper body of a woman and the tail of a fish, found in folklore across the world.

11. Fairy: Supernatural beings in European folklore, often depicted as small, human-like creatures with magical powers.

12. Werewolf: A human with the ability to transform into a wolf or a wolf-like creature, especially during a full moon.

13. Minotaur: A creature from Greek mythology with the body of a man and the head of a bull, dwelling in the Labyrinth of Crete.

14. Loch Ness Monster: A large aquatic creature said to inhabit Loch Ness in Scotland, often described as resembling a plesiosaur.

15. Sphinx: In Greek mythology, a creature with the body of a lion, the head of a human, and sometimes wings, known for posing riddles.

16. Centaur: A creature from Greek mythology with the upper body of a human and the lower body of a horse.

17. Hydra: A multi-headed serpent from Greek mythology, with the ability to regenerate two heads for each one cut off.

18. Cerberus: The three-headed dog guarding the entrance to the Underworld in Greek mythology.

19. Mothman: A creature reportedly seen in Point Pleasant, West Virginia, described as a large, winged humanoid with glowing red eyes.

20. Kitsune: In Japanese folklore, a fox spirit with the ability to shapeshift into a human and possessing magical abilities.

Lost Treasures

1. El Dorado: A mythical city of gold supposedly located in South America, inspiring numerous expeditions and searches.

2. The Amber Room: A chamber decorated with amber panels, gold leaf, and mirrors, lost during World War II after being stolen by Nazi Germany.

3. The Lost Dutchman's Mine: A legendary gold mine believed to be located in the Superstition Mountains of Arizona.

4. Treasure of the Knights Templar: Rumored to include the Holy Grail and other religious artifacts, said to be hidden by the Knights Templar.

5. The San Miguel Treasure: A Spanish galleon carrying vast riches that sank off the coast of Florida in 1715.

6. The Florentine Diamond: A large yellow diamond that disappeared after the fall of the Austrian Empire at the end of World War I.

7. The Lost Treasure of King John: In 1216, King John of England allegedly lost a treasure trove in the Wash, a tidal estuary in East Anglia.

8. Oak Island Money Pit: A site on Oak Island in Nova Scotia where treasure hunters have been searching for buried treasure since the 18th century.

9. The Treasure of Lima: A vast treasure hidden by Captain William Thompson in 1820 to avoid capture by Spanish forces.

10. The Fabergé Eggs: Fifty-two Imperial eggs made for the Russian Tsars, with several still missing after the Russian Revolution.

11. The Nazi Gold Train: Rumored to be filled with gold, jewels, and other valuables, believed to be hidden in a tunnel in Poland.

12. Captain Kidd's Treasure: The pirate William Kidd is said to have buried a treasure worth millions, sparking numerous searches.

13. Yamashita's Gold: A treasure supposedly hidden in the Philippines by Japanese General Tomoyuki Yamashita during World War II.

14. The Cahuenga Pass Treasure: A cache of gold coins buried in Los Angeles during the Mexican-American War.

15. Blackbeard's Treasure: The infamous pirate Blackbeard is believed to have hidden a vast fortune, never to be found.

16. The Treasure of the Nuestra Señora de Atocha: A Spanish galleon that sank off the Florida Keys in 1622, with much of its treasure still missing.

17. The Ark of the Covenant: A gold-covered wooden chest described in biblical texts, said to hold the stone tablets of the Ten Commandments.

18. The Patiala Necklace: A necklace made by Cartier for the Maharaja of Patiala, with many of its jewels missing since 1948.

19. The Lost Inca Gold: A vast treasure hidden by the Incas from Spanish conquistadors, said to be in the mountains of Ecuador.

20. The Treasure of the Llanganates: Gold and valuables hidden by the Incas in the Llanganates Mountains of Ecuador to keep them from Spanish conquerors.

Unusual Professions

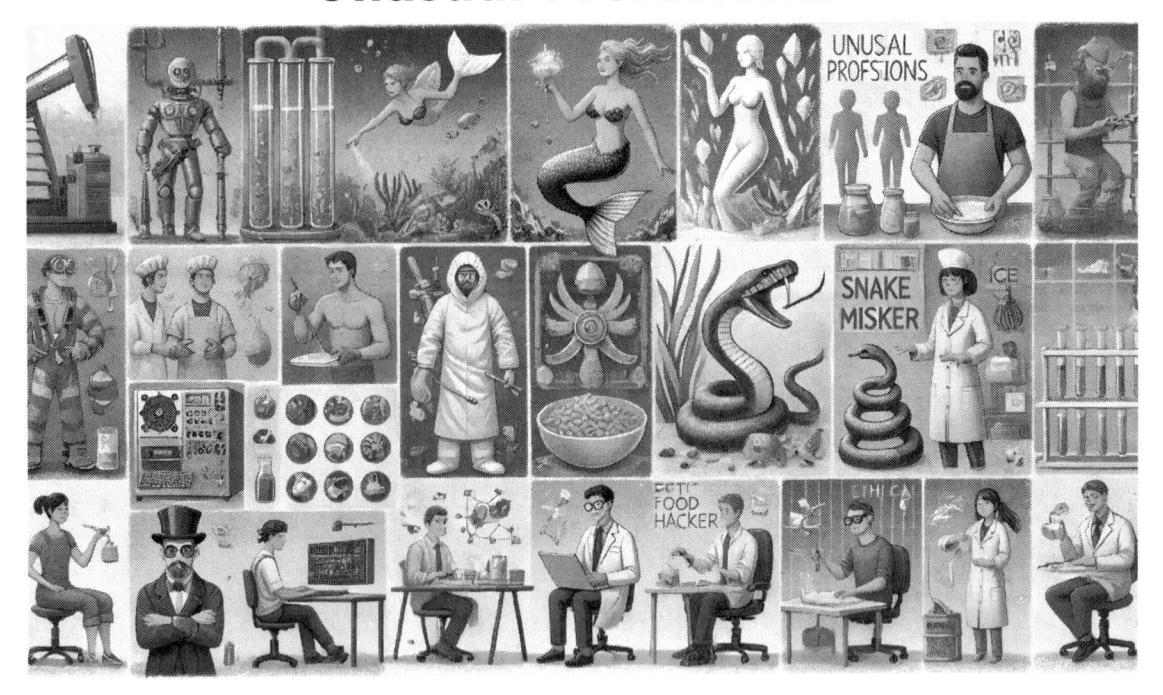

1. Professional Cuddler: Offers therapeutic touch sessions to clients for relaxation and emotional support.

2. Pet Food Taster: Ensures the quality and taste of pet food products, often using human taste buds to evaluate them.

3. Iceberg Mover: Diverts icebergs away from oil rigs and shipping lanes to prevent collisions.

4. Professional Mourner: Hired to attend funerals and express grief, a tradition in some cultures to show respect for the deceased.

5. Odor Judge: Assesses the effectiveness of odor-control products by smelling armpits, feet, and other test areas.

6. Waterslide Tester: Tests water slides for safety, speed, and fun factor, ensuring they meet standards before public use.

7. Foley Artist: Creates sound effects for films and television using everyday objects to mimic real-world sounds.

8. Snake Milker: Extracts venom from snakes for use in medical research and antivenom production.

9. Face Feeler: Employed by skincare companies to assess the effectiveness of products by feeling the faces of test subjects.

10. Golf Ball Diver: Retrieves lost golf balls from water hazards on golf courses, often reselling them.

11. Line Stand-In: Waits in long lines for events, product releases, or other occasions on behalf of clients.

12. Professional Bridesmaid: Hired to assist brides with wedding planning and day-of coordination, often blending in with the bridal party.

13. Living Statue: Performs as a statue in public places, staying still for long periods to entertain passersby.

14. Human Scarecrow: Employed to scare birds away from crops by standing in fields and making noise.

15. Gumologist: Specializes in the study and development of chewing gum flavors and textures.

16. Dog Surfing Instructor: Teaches dogs how to surf, often participating in dog surfing competitions.

17. Virtual Gold Farmer: Earns in-game currency in online games to sell for real money to other players.

18. Ethical Hacker: Hired by companies to find and fix security vulnerabilities in their systems.

19. Professional Whistler: Performs whistling at events or in music recordings, showcasing exceptional control and range.

20. Professional Mermaid: Dresses as a mermaid for entertainment at events, aquariums, and underwater performances.

Remarkable Survivals

1. Aron Ralston: Trapped by a boulder while hiking, he amputated his own arm to free himself after five days in 2003.

2. Juliane Koepcke: Survived a plane crash in the Amazon rainforest in 1971 and trekked through the jungle for 11 days to safety.

3. Joe Simpson: Survived a fall into a crevasse while climbing in the Andes, managing to crawl back to base camp with a broken leg.

4. Poon Lim: Survived 133 days at sea on a life raft during World War II after his ship was torpedoed.

5. Hugh Glass: Mauled by a bear and left for dead by his companions in 1823, he crawled 200 miles to safety.

6. Steven Callahan: Drifted 76 days in an inflatable raft in the Atlantic Ocean after his sailboat sank in 1981.

7. Beck Weathers: Survived severe frostbite and near-death conditions during the 1996 Mount Everest disaster.

8. Ricky Megee: Survived for 71 days in the Australian Outback by eating insects and drinking rainwater after being stranded.

9. Louis Zamperini: Survived 47 days on a raft in the Pacific Ocean during World War II, then endured two years in Japanese POW camps.

10. Aaron Harris: Survived a shark attack while surfing in Australia, managing to paddle back to shore despite severe injuries.

11. Alexander Selkirk: The real-life inspiration for Robinson Crusoe, he survived four years on a deserted island in the Pacific Ocean.

12. Deborah Scaling Kiley: Survived five days in a lifeboat in the Atlantic Ocean after her yacht sank, facing dehydration and shark attacks.

13. Satoru Uchida: Survived 43 days trapped in a collapsed tunnel in Japan in 1986 with limited food and water.

14. Roy Sullivan: Struck by lightning seven times throughout his life and survived each strike.

15. Natalia Molchanova: Russian freediver who survived being trapped under ice during a training dive, rescued by her team.

16. Paul Templer: Survived a hippopotamus attack in Africa, sustaining severe injuries but managing to escape.

17. Michael Benson: Survived 11 days adrift in the Gulf of Mexico after his fishing boat capsized, living off rainwater and raw fish.

18. Annette Herfkens: The sole survivor of a plane crash in the Vietnamese jungle in 1992, surviving eight days before being rescued.

19. Hiroo Onoda: A Japanese soldier who survived for 29 years in the Philippine jungle, unaware that World War II had ended.

20. Frane Selak: A Croatian man who survived seven near-death experiences, including plane crashes, train derailments, and car accidents.

Historical Artifacts

1. Rosetta Stone: Discovered in 1799, this stone helped decipher Egyptian hieroglyphs with its inscriptions in three scripts.

2. Dead Sea Scrolls: Ancient Jewish texts found in the Qumran Caves, dating back to the 3rd century BCE.

3. Terracotta Army: Thousands of life-sized clay soldiers buried with China's first emperor, Qin Shi Huang.

4. King Tutankhamun's Tomb: Discovered in 1922, it contained a wealth of artifacts and the intact sarcophagus of the boy king.

5. Mona Lisa: Painted by Leonardo da Vinci, it is one of the most famous and valuable artworks in the world.

6. Antikythera Mechanism: An ancient Greek analog computer used to predict astronomical positions, discovered in a shipwreck.

7. The Code of Hammurabi: One of the oldest deciphered writings of significant length, detailing Babylonian laws.

8. The Bayeux Tapestry: An embroidered cloth depicting the events leading up to the Norman conquest of England.

9. The Mask of Agamemnon: A gold funeral mask discovered at Mycenae, Greece, dating back to the 16th century BCE.

10. The Gutenberg Bible: The first major book printed using movable type, marking the start of the "Gutenberg Revolution."

11. The Venus de Milo: An ancient Greek statue believed to depict Aphrodite, notable for its missing arms.

12. The Book of Kells: An illuminated manuscript Gospel book in Latin, created by Celtic monks around 800 CE.

13. The Shroud of Turin: A length of linen cloth bearing the image of a man, believed by some to be Jesus Christ.

14. The Elgin Marbles: A collection of classical Greek marble sculptures that were part of the Parthenon and other buildings on the Acropolis of Athens.

15. The Hope Diamond: A large, blue diamond with a history of ownership by various monarchs and a reputation for bringing bad luck.

16. The Spear of Destiny: A relic said to be the spear that pierced the side of Jesus during his crucifixion.

17. The Sutton Hoo Helmet: An ornate Anglo-Saxon helmet found in a ship burial, symbolizing the wealth and power of its owner.

18. The Crown Jewels: The ceremonial regalia and vestments worn by the kings and queens of the United Kingdom.

19. The Declaration of Independence: The original manuscript declaring the Thirteen Colonies' independence from Britain.

20. The Moai Statues: Monolithic human figures carved by the Rapa Nui people on Easter Island.

Sports Trivia

1. The Olympics: The modern Olympic Games began in 1896 in Athens, Greece, with 14 countries participating.

2. FIFA World Cup: The first FIFA World Cup was held in 1930 in Uruguay, with the host nation winning the tournament.

3. Michael Phelps: Holds the record for the most Olympic gold medals, with a total of 23.

4. Wimbledon: The oldest tennis tournament in the world, first held in 1877 in London.

5. Super Bowl: The most-watched annual sporting event in the United States, first held in 1967.

6. Usain Bolt: The fastest man in the world, holding the world records for the 100m and 200m sprints.

7. The Tour de France: The most prestigious cycling race in the world, first held in 1903.

8. Jackie Robinson: Broke the color barrier in Major League Baseball in 1947, playing for the Brooklyn Dodgers.

9. The Boston Marathon: The world's oldest annual marathon, first run in 1897.

10. Muhammad Ali: Considered one of the greatest boxers of all time, known for his charisma and skill in the ring.

11. Rugby World Cup: The first Rugby World Cup was held in 1987, with New Zealand winning the tournament.

12. The Stanley Cup: The championship trophy awarded annually to the NHL playoff winner, first awarded in 1893.

13. The Green Jacket: Awarded to the winner of The Masters golf tournament, first awarded in 1949.

14. The Triple Crown: Winning the Kentucky Derby, Preakness Stakes, and Belmont Stakes in a single season, achieved by 13 horses as of 2021.

15. Pelé: Considered one of the greatest soccer players of all time, winning three FIFA World Cups with Brazil.

16. The Grand Slam: Winning all four major tennis tournaments (Australian Open, French Open, Wimbledon, and US Open) in a single calendar year.

17. The Miracle on Ice: The U.S. men's ice hockey team's victory over the Soviet Union in the 1980 Winter Olympics.

18. The Indianapolis 500: An annual car race held at the Indianapolis Motor Speedway, first run in 1911.

19. Serena Williams: One of the greatest female tennis players of all time, with 23 Grand Slam singles titles.

20. The Heisman Trophy: Awarded annually to the most outstanding player in college football, first awarded in 1935.

Intellectual Property

1. Patent: A form of intellectual property that grants the inventor exclusive rights to their invention for a limited time, usually 20 years.

2. Copyright: Protects original works of authorship, such as literary, dramatic, musical, and artistic works, for the life of the author plus 70 years.

3. Trademark: A symbol, word, or phrase legally registered or established by use as representing a company or product.

4. Trade Secret: Information that companies keep secret to give them an advantage over their competitors, such as recipes or manufacturing processes.

5. First Patent: The first U.S. patent was granted on July 31, 1790, to Samuel Hopkins for a process of making potash, an ingredient used in fertilizer.

6. Public Domain: Works that are not protected by intellectual property laws and are available for public use, often because the copyright has expired.

7. Patent Trolls: Entities that buy patents, not to produce products, but to sue others for infringement, often viewed negatively.

8. Creative Commons: A nonprofit organization that provides free licenses that creators can use to share their work while retaining some rights.

9. Fair Use: A legal doctrine that allows limited use of copyrighted material without permission from the rights holders for purposes like criticism, comment, news reporting, teaching, scholarship, and research.

10. Trademark Dilution: The weakening of a famous trademark's distinctiveness and reputation due to unauthorized use.

11. Geographical Indications: Signs used on products that have a specific geographical origin and possess qualities or a reputation due to that origin, such as Champagne or Roquefort cheese.

12. Moral Rights: Rights of creators to protect their personal and reputational connection to their work, even after the copyright has been transferred.

13. Patent Cooperation Treaty (PCT): An international patent law treaty that provides a unified procedure for filing patent applications in multiple countries.

14. Orphan Works: Works for which the copyright owner cannot be located, creating challenges for those who wish to use the work legally.

15. Berne Convention: An international agreement governing copyright, which requires its signatories to recognize the copyright of works of authors from other signatory countries.

16. Intellectual Property Office (IPO): Government bodies responsible for overseeing the registration and enforcement of IP rights, such as the U.S. Patent and Trademark Office.

17. Patent Infringement: The violation of a patent holder's rights by unauthorized use, production, or sale of the patented invention.

18. Software Patents: Controversial patents that protect software innovations, with debates over their impact on innovation and competition.

19. Digital Rights Management (DRM): Technologies used by copyright holders to control how their digital content is used and distributed.

20. Plant Variety Protection: Intellectual property rights granted to breeders of new varieties of plants that are distinct, uniform, and stable.

Ethnography

1. Fieldwork: The primary method of ethnographic research, involving extended stays in the community being studied to observe and participate in daily life.

2. Participant Observation: A key ethnographic technique where researchers immerse themselves in the community to gain a deeper understanding of their practices and beliefs.

3. Ethnographic Interviews: In-depth, open-ended interviews conducted with members of the community to gather detailed information about their lives and perspectives.

4. Thick Description: A term coined by Clifford Geertz, referring to detailed, nuanced descriptions of social actions that provide context and meaning.

5. Emic Perspective: An insider's view of a culture, focusing on the intrinsic cultural distinctions meaningful to the members of the society.

6. Etic Perspective: An outsider's view of a culture, emphasizing the observer's understanding and categorization of social phenomena.

7. Autoethnography: A form of ethnographic writing where the researcher uses self-reflection to connect personal experience to wider cultural, social, and political meanings.

8. Ethnographic Film: A documentary genre that visually represents the practices, rituals, and everyday life of different cultures.

9. Multi-Sited Ethnography: Research that follows a topic or social issue across multiple locations, examining how it manifests in different contexts.

10. Reflexivity: The practice of reflecting on one's own role and impact as a researcher, acknowledging biases and the influence of personal background.

11. Ethical Considerations: Ensuring informed consent, protecting confidentiality, and avoiding harm to participants are crucial in ethnographic research.

12. Ethnography of Communication: Studies how language is used in different social contexts, focusing on speech events, genres, and communicative competence.

13. Life History Method: Collecting detailed personal narratives from individuals to understand their experiences and the broader cultural context.

14. Visual Ethnography: Incorporates photography, video, and other visual media to capture and analyze cultural practices.

15. Digital Ethnography: The study of online communities and digital interactions, also known as virtual ethnography or netnography.

16. Cultural Relativism: The principle of understanding and interpreting cultural practices within their own context, without imposing one's own cultural biases.

17. Ethnographic Monographs: Detailed, book-length studies that provide comprehensive accounts of a particular culture or social phenomenon.

18. Salvage Ethnography: Early ethnographic work aimed at documenting cultures and practices believed to be disappearing due to modernization and colonization.

19. Key Informants: Individuals within the community who provide valuable insights and assistance to the researcher due to their knowledge and position.

20. Institutional Ethnography: Examines the everyday practices of institutions, focusing on how people's actions are shaped by and shape organizational structures.

Transhumanism

1. Definition: Transhumanism is an intellectual movement advocating for the use of technology to enhance human physical and cognitive abilities.

2. Singularity: A hypothetical future point when technological growth becomes uncontrollable and irreversible, resulting in unforeseeable changes to human civilization.

3. Cryonics: The practice of preserving individuals at extremely low temperatures with the hope of future revival and medical advancements.

4. Biohacking: The DIY biology movement, where individuals experiment with technology and biology to enhance their own bodies and minds.

5. Mind Uploading: The theoretical process of scanning a human brain and transferring its consciousness to a digital medium or artificial body.

6. Genetic Engineering: The manipulation of an organism's genes using biotechnology, potentially allowing for the elimination of genetic diseases and enhancement of human abilities.

7. Cyborgs: Beings with both organic and biomechatronic body parts, enhancing their physical or cognitive abilities.

8. Wearable Technology: Devices like smartwatches and fitness trackers that monitor and enhance bodily functions and health.

9. Artificial Intelligence (AI): The development of computer systems that can perform tasks typically requiring human intelligence, such as decision-making and problem-solving.

10. Nanotechnology: The manipulation of matter on an atomic or molecular scale, which could lead to advanced medical treatments and human enhancement.

11. Life Extension: Research and interventions aimed at extending human lifespan and delaying the aging process.

12. Augmented Reality (AR): Technology that overlays digital information onto the physical world, enhancing human perception and interaction with the environment.

13. Brain-Computer Interfaces (BCIs): Systems that enable direct communication between the brain and an external device, potentially restoring lost functions or enhancing abilities.

14. Exoskeletons: Wearable robotic devices that enhance physical capabilities, aiding mobility and strength for disabled individuals and workers.

15. Ethical Considerations: Debates surrounding the moral implications of human enhancement, including issues of inequality, consent, and the definition of humanity.

16. Designer Babies: The concept of using genetic engineering to select or alter traits in unborn children, raising ethical and societal concerns.

17. Smart Drugs (Nootropics): Substances claimed to improve cognitive function, memory, creativity, or motivation in healthy individuals.

18. Virtual Reality (VR): Immersive digital environments that can simulate real or imagined experiences, potentially revolutionizing education, entertainment, and therapy.

19. Posthumanism: A philosophy that explores what comes after humanity as we currently understand it, considering the implications of advanced technology and human enhancement.

20. Human-Machine Integration: The blending of biological and artificial components to create enhanced humans, often seen as a core goal of transhumanism.

Dinosaurs

1. Existence Period: Dinosaurs roamed the Earth for approximately 165 million years, from the Triassic period (around 230 million years ago) to the end of the Cretaceous period (about 65 million years ago).

2. Discovery: The first dinosaur fossils were recognized in the early 19th century. Sir Richard Owen coined the term "dinosaur" in 1842, which means "terrible lizard" in Greek.

3. Largest Dinosaur: The Argentinosaurus is believed to be the largest dinosaur, possibly reaching lengths of up to 100 feet and weighing around 100 tons.

4. Smallest Dinosaur: The Microraptor, a tiny feathered dinosaur, measured about 2.5 feet in length and weighed approximately 2.2 pounds.

5. Feathered Dinosaurs: Many theropod dinosaurs, including the Velociraptor, had feathers. This discovery supports the evolutionary link between dinosaurs and modern birds.

6. Dinosaur Eggs: Fossilized dinosaur eggs have been found on every continent, providing insight into the reproductive habits of these ancient creatures.

7. Bipedal and Quadrupedal: Dinosaurs were diverse in their locomotion. Some, like the Tyrannosaurus rex, were bipedal (walked on two legs), while others, like the Brachiosaurus, were quadrupedal (walked on four legs).

8. Meteor Impact Theory: The most widely accepted theory for the mass extinction of dinosaurs is the impact of a large asteroid or comet, creating the Chicxulub crater in present-day Mexico.

9. Herbivores and Carnivores: Dinosaurs were divided into herbivores (plant-eaters) like the Triceratops and carnivores (meat-eaters) like the Allosaurus.

10. Dinosaur Claws: Therizinosaurus had the longest claws of any known animal, measuring up to 3 feet in length.

11. Dinosaur Vision: Some dinosaurs, like the Troodon, had large eyes and likely had excellent vision, possibly even better than modern birds.

12. T. rex Bite Force: The Tyrannosaurus rex had one of the strongest bite forces of any animal, estimated at around 12,800 pounds of force.

13. Dinosaur Brains: The Stegosaurus had a brain the size of a walnut, despite its large body size, leading some scientists to speculate it had a second "brain" in its hips to control its movements.

14. Oldest Dinosaur: The Eoraptor, discovered in Argentina, is one of the oldest known dinosaurs, living around 231 million years ago.

15. Dinosaur Fossils: Dinosaur fossils have been found on all seven continents, including Antarctica.

16. Sauropods: Some of the largest dinosaurs, like the Diplodocus and Apatosaurus, were sauropods, characterized by their long necks and tails.

17. Cretaceous Period: The Cretaceous period, the last era of the dinosaurs, saw the greatest diversity of dinosaur species.

18. Dinosaur Speed: The Velociraptor was likely one of the fastest dinosaurs, capable of running at speeds up to 40 miles per hour.

19. Armored Dinosaurs: Dinosaurs like the Ankylosaurus had heavily armored bodies and tail clubs to defend against predators.

20. Dinosaur Nesting: Some dinosaurs, like the Maiasaura, were known for their nesting behavior, caring for their young after they hatched.

Printed in Great Britain
by Amazon